THE CROSS STITCH KIT

THE CROSS STITCH KIT

25 Elegant and Easy-to-Make Projects
for Every Room in the House

Juliet Bawden

WATSON-GUPTILL PUBLICATIONS/NEW YORK

THIS BOOK IS DEDICATED TO ILDIKO AND FERI, WITH LOVE

Editor: Heather Dewhurst
Designer: Paul Calver
Styling: Labeena Ishaque
Charts: Jack Moxley
Photographer: Jon Bouchier

The cushion shown on p.61 originally appeared in
The Cushion Book, by Juliet Bawden, and is included in
this book by courtesy of New Holland Publishers.

First published in the United States in 1997 by
Watson-Guptill Publications,
a division of BPI Communications, Inc.,
1515 Broadway, New York, N.Y. 10036

Library of Congress Catalog Card Number: 97-060927

ISBN 0-8230-1127-5

First published in 1997 by
HarperCollins*Publishers*, London

Color origination by Colourscan, Singapore
Manufactured in China

First printing, 1997

1 2 3 4 5 6 7 8 9 / 05 04 03 02 01 00 99 98 97

CONTENTS

Cross-Stitch Basics

Cross stitch is probably the simplest yet most versatile of all embroidery stitches. When, as a child, I was first called upon to sew at school, a simple cross-stitch patch was the first thing I made, using a large-weave piece of Aida fabric and wool yarn. Although it is often the first stitch learned in needlework, cross stitch can also be used to create the most elaborate of embroidered cloths, transforming plain sheets of fabric into wonderfully patterned and decorative textiles. This simple stitch, consisting of a tiny cross, can create straightforward symmetrical patterns or vast pictorial visions.

  Cross stitch was one of the first methods of needlework used to hold together animal skins for shelter and clothing. However, over a great many centuries, the practicality of the first cross stitch has been replaced by the purely decorative cross stitch. From the cloth remnants of Ancient Egypt and the Chinese white gauzes with dark blue cross stitches, to the Scandinavian red embroidery on white linens, we can see that this particular stitch has been used throughout the world and throughout time by people from all walks of life.

Tools and Materials

Listed below are some of the essential tools and materials for cross stitch as well as some other useful aids for your work.

FABRICS

In order to work cross stitch you need a material with an even weave—that is, a fabric which has the same number of threads over a given distance, both vertically and horizontally. There are many kinds of evenweave fabrics, including linens and cottons.

Aida

This is a cotton fabric specifically woven for counted cross-stitch work. It is excellent for beginners as the warp and weft threads are grouped together; this creates clearly defined holes through which the needle can pass. Aida fabric is available in 8, 11, 14, 16, and 18 blocks per 1in (2.5cm); this is also known as 8-count, 11-count, etc. When stitching Aida, one block of fabric responds to one square on a chart.

Aida band (edging)

There is a huge variety of Aida band styles available for cross

Aida band can be plain and straight, or scalloped.

stitch, ranging from 1in (2.5cm) to 6in (15cm) wide. Aida band is available in rolls, so that it can be cut to whatever length is required. Although the most popular colors are white and off-white, it comes in many pastel shades with scalloped or woven edges. Aida band is also available in linen.

Evenweave

This is a very popular fabric for cross stitch. It can be obtained in a variety of sizes, thread counts, types, and a range of usually pale, pastel colors. Fabrics range from 10 threads to 36 threads per 1in (2.5cm).

Hardanger

This is a type of evenweave fabric where pairs of threads are woven together. It is used for cross stitch and blackwork embroidery, which is a type of embroidery stitched on a black background.

Binca

This is an evenweave fabric with a count of 6 threads per 1in (2.5cm). It is large and bold and suitable for children who are learning embroidery and for those who have difficulty working with small stitches.

Linen

Linen has irregularities in the weave which occur naturally. This does look beautiful but it

Evenweave fabric is available in many sizes.

can make the fabric difficult to work on. So it is recommended that experienced stitchers rather than novices use this type of close-weave linen. Linen is available in most colors, but the best colors to work on with cross stitch are white, ivory, cream, and raw or unbleached shades.

Waste canvas

Waste canvas is a very loosely woven canvas with thick, stiff threads held together with water-soluble starch. This sewing aid assists in spacing and sizing stitches on fabric where the weave is difficult to see. The waste canvas is basted onto the fabric, and then the cross stitch is worked on top of and through both the waste canvas and the fabric. When the design is finished, the waste canvas is cut away. The remaining canvas is dampened to release the starch, and then the threads are very carefully pulled away, strand by strand, with tweezers.

Fabric preparation

If you are working on fabric that is liable to shrink, wash it first and allow the shrinkage to pass,

before doing any work on it. If the fabric has been folded or is creased, steam iron it before cutting or beginning to embroider, as this will make measuring, pinning, and basting easier. For most projects it is necessary to find the middle of the piece of fabric. Mark this both lengthways and widthways using basting stitches in a contrasting color of thread. Where the two lines of stitching cross is the center point of the cloth.

THREADS AND YARNS

There are several types of threads that you can use for cross stitch. Six-stranded cotton is most commonly used, but you can use Danish flower thread if you prefer more natural colors, perlé for a silky look or coton à broder for a duller finish.

Stranded cotton (floss)

All the projects in this book have been worked in DMC stranded cottons. Stranded cotton comes in six strands of mercerized cotton, which are usually divided before stitching begins. Sometimes, three strands are used, and sometimes two; this is generally dependent

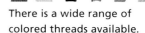

There is a wide range of colored threads available.

on the size of the weave of the fabric you work upon. As a general guide, on 10 to 16-count fabric use two or three strands, on 16 to 20-count use two strands, and on counts of more than 20 use one strand.

You can prepare your threads before starting to stitch, by using a thread selector card. These are available from haberdashery stores or you can easily make your own. To do this, punch a row of holes down the sides of a piece of card. Cut the embroidery cottons into manageable lengths (16-20in/40-50cm long), double them and thread them through the holes, securing with a simple loop knot. Mark the shade number of the color next to the threads.

Danish flower thread
This is a matte-finished thread made of combed cotton. It is often indivisible or has only two intertwined strands. The range of colors available is not as wide as the colors for stranded cotton, but it has a more natural palette. The color range and its matte finish make this type of thread suitable for work on linen and wool. On counts of 14 to 20 use two threads, and on counts of 20 or more use one thread.

Perlé (pearl cotton)
Perlé is a thick silky thread which has a shiny finish when stitches are close together. This twisted two-ply thread is available in three thicknesses, and is ideal for embroidery on coarse, heavyweight fabrics and for bold patterns.

Coton à broder
This is a five-ply, dull-surfaced thread which is also used on heavyweight fabrics.

EQUIPMENT
Other necessary requirements are scissors, an embroidery needle, pins, a ruler and tape measure, scalpel, and a frame to hold the material taut while working. You will also need a pattern to follow, as all counted designs are made up of squares.

Scissors
You will need three pairs of scissors in your cross-stitching kit. Dressmaker's scissors are needed for cutting cloth and a small pair of fine, pointed embroidery scissors are essential for cutting threads and trimming delicate areas of work. Never use fabric scissors for cutting paper as this blunts them.

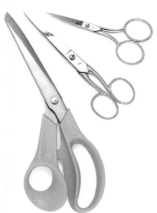

Sharp scissors are essential for cross-stitch work.

Needles
Round-ended tapestry needles are the most suitable for working cross stitch as they pass easily through holes without snagging or splitting the stitches. They are available in different sizes, ranging from 13 to 26; the most common for cross stitch are sizes 24 and 26.

For basting and finishing projects a range of sewing needles will be required. Always avoid leaving needles in your work when it is put away as they may mark the fabric. The best way to keep needles together and avoid losing them, is to keep a small magnet at hand and keep the needles stuck to it when they are not in use.

Pins
You may need dressmaker's pins for marking before basting, and instead of basting when the project is really simple.

Measuring aids
A ruler and a tape measure will be needed for measuring fabric, seam allowances, the weave on fabrics, and for ruling lines.

Frames and hoops
Some designers never use a frame and dislike the whole idea of it. Others believe that in order to achieve a neat finish it is essential to use a frame. You can, if you wish, just stretch your material over an old picture frame using drawing pins or a staple gun to secure the fabric to the frame.

Tambour or ring frame
This is often known as an embroidery hoop and is made up of two rings, one inside the other. The outside ring has a screw fitting which is tightened to enable the ring to hold the fabric firmly in place. Tambour frames are available in several

Use an embroidery hoop to keep the fabric taut.

sizes ranging from 4in (10cm) to 15in (38cm); the larger ones are more often used for quilting rather than embroidery.

Rotating frame
This frame is composed of two top rollers or bars, with tapes attached, and two side pieces. The rollers slot into the side pieces and are held securely by pegs or butterfly-screws. The tape length regulates the size of the frame. Some frames are free-standing while others clip on to the arm of a chair.

Stitch guide
A stitch guide will help you to follow a chart more accurately. The stitch guide is positioned on the chart and aligned with the row of stitches you are working, to ensure you do not skip a line. As you complete an area of the chart, you simply reposition the stitch guide.

A stitch guide will help you to follow a chart accurately.

Cross-Stitch Techniques

This section explains how to work cross stitches and how to follow a pattern chart.

Beginning your work

An experienced cross stitcher will judge a piece of work not by the front, but by the back of it. It should be as neat as the front.

When you begin stitching, never tie a knot; instead, pull the needle through from the front of the fabric, leaving an end of about 2in (5cm) on the right side. Hold this end securely while working the first stitch. When several stitches have been completed, thread this end on a needle, push it through to the back of the cloth and weave it through the worked stitches.

Working cross stitch

Cross stitch is generally worked in one of two ways. The first way, which is the quicker method, is to work along a row in one direction with half stitches, and then come back in the other direction making the other half of each of the stitches. The second way is to make rows of complete stitches; this is easiest when working large blocks of color. But whichever method you choose to follow, the most important thing to remember is that the top of the stitches should slant in the same direction to prevent the work from looking untidy.

Large areas are best worked in horizontal rows. When working diagonally, complete a cross before starting the next stitch. When filling in an area, start at the widest section and work toward a narrow or tapered part of the design.

Using the charts

Each square on the charts accompanying the projects in this book represents one cross stitch. Thread colors are listed with each chart. Whereas the charts for all the new projects in the book are exact replicas of the projects, the charts for antique projects, such as the throw, runner, bordered tablecloth, linen towels, linen sash, and sampler, have been altered and adjusted in some cases either to simplify the design, or to remove errors made in the working of the original piece. On these projects your completed design will be as shown on the chart and not exactly as on the original piece. The pieces stitched on gingham will look different from the charts when worked. When working on gingham, one square of the gingham equals one square on the chart.

Before you begin stitching, mark the center point on the chart and mark the center of your fabric by basting two lines of stitches, one vertical and one horizontal, running from edge to edge of the fabric. It is often easiest to begin stitching from the center of the design. Use the center marks as reference points when counting squares and threads to position your design.

Changing dimensions

You can work counted cross stitch on any count of fabric you like; although I have given numbers of holes per 1in (2.5cm), you can in fact work any design on more or less holes. The rule is that the number of stitches in a width of pattern divided by the number of holes per 1in (2.5cm) equals the finished size of the work shown. The more holes per 1in (2.5cm), the smaller the piece of work will be; the less holes per 1in (2.5cm), the larger the piece of work will be.

To Work Cross Stitch in Rows

1. Work from left to right making half crosses in the same direction.

2. Work from right to left making the second half of each cross over the first row of crosses.

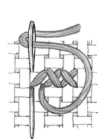

To Work Single Cross Stitches

1. Bring the needle up at point 1 and insert it at point 2 to make a half cross stitch.

2. Bring the needle up at point 3 and insert it at point 4 to cover the first stitch and complete the cross.

LIVING ROOMS

Cross-stitched accessories add an individual and creative touch to any living room, whether it is small and cottagey or large and modern. In this chapter are featured a curtain tie-back embroidered in bright scarlet on a crisp white Aida fabric, a runner embroidered with a heavy wool tapestry yarn on an aged cream linen, and a huge red and white sofa throw, which was made by a friend's grandmother. For the novice there are some quick and easy needle cases to stitch; the size of the actual cross-stitch piece on each measures no more than a few inches.

Curtain tie-back

Curtain tie-backs are traditional subjects for cross stitch and can be made in a huge array of shapes and sizes to suit your particular curtains. The tie-back featured here is embroidered in a pattern of interlocking diamonds and swirls, but you could stitch any pattern you like; as the area to be stitched is not very large, the stitching can be completed fairly quickly. The embroidered tie-back is then finished off with matching tassels.

MATERIALS

For the cross-stitch design:

two pieces of 11-count, white Aida fabric, 19 x 6in (48 x 15cm)

dark cotton thread

sewing needle

3 skeins of red (DMC 321) stranded cotton

tapestry needle

Other materials:

dressmaker's scissors

pins

3in (7.5cm) square of cardboard

2 skeins of red (DMC 321) stranded cotton

white cotton thread

SIZE

The completed design measures 16½ x 5in (42 x 13cm) at the widest points.

▲ To make the tie-back, the cross-stitch design is backed on to another piece of Aida fabric and sewn neatly around the edges. The tie-back is then completed with a matching tassel tie. Tassels can be bought ready made or you can construct your own using embroidery thread, following the instructions on page 14.

▶ The tie-back design is made up of diamonds, both interlocking and independent. The use of bright red on white is often found in European cross stitch.

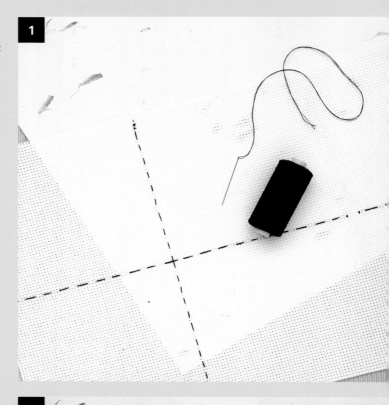

Getting started

The chart on pages 16 and 17 illustrates the entire length of the tie-back. It is worth cutting a remnant of fabric to this size and using it as a test piece to make sure that the tie-back is the correct size for your curtain. It will be easier to work the cross stitch if the Aida is stretched across a frame or hoop.

Working the cross stitch

1 Referring to the chart, work out the center point of the design. Then mark the center of the Aida fabric with two lines of basting stitches in a dark cotton thread, one vertical and one horizontal, running from edge to edge of the fabric. Where these two lines cross is the center of the fabric. Use these stitching lines as guidelines when you stitch.

2 Starting at the center and following the chart, begin to stitch the design using two strands of red stranded cotton in the needle. Work outwards to each side of the fabric to build up the pattern. When the stitching is complete, press the wrong side of the fabric with a warm iron.

3 **Making up the tie-back**
Using sharp dressmaker's scissors to avoid puckering and fraying the material, cut away the excess Aida fabric around the stitched pattern, leaving a ⅝in (1.5cm) seam allowance. Make the piece narrower at the middle and slightly curved at the two ends.

4 Place this shaped piece of Aida fabric on top of a second piece of Aida, and pin the two together. Cut the second piece to match.

5 Place the two pieces of Aida fabric wrong sides together, so that the cross stitch is facing outwards. Fold in the edges and pin them to secure. Then overstitch all the way around.

6 Make up two tassels. For each tassel, wind one skein of embroidery cotton around a square piece of cardboard, until you are left with 12in (30cm). Thread this end through a needle, then thread the needle underneath the bulk of the wound cotton. Secure and knot this end, then cut through the cotton at the other end of the cardboard. Bind the top end until the tassel seems secure, then thread the needle and cotton up through the center of the tassel. Make a second tassel in the same way and sew them to each end of the curtain tie-back. Hold the ends of the tie-back together around the curtain by tying the two tassels.

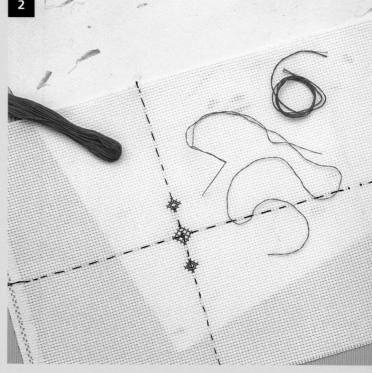

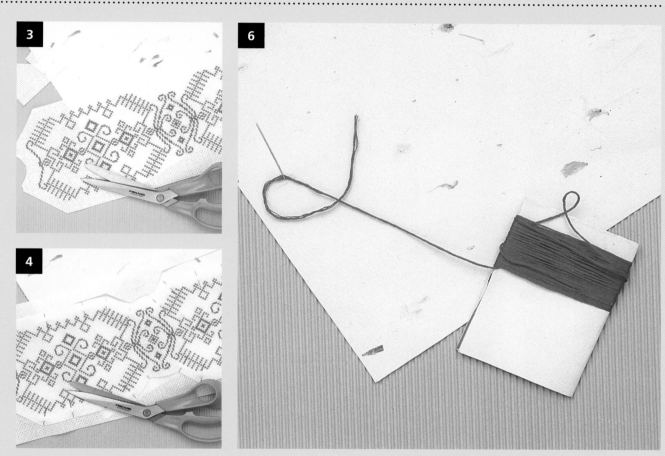

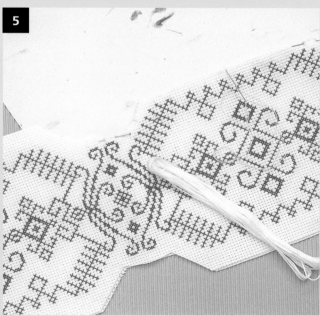

TIP BOX

To make a smaller tie-back, use Aida fabric with a higher count. This means that you will have more stitches per inch, and the diamond design will be smaller. Alternatively, you can extend the length of the tie-back by repeating the central design and extending the top and bottom borders.

THREAD COLOR

		Anchor	DMC
	Red	47	321

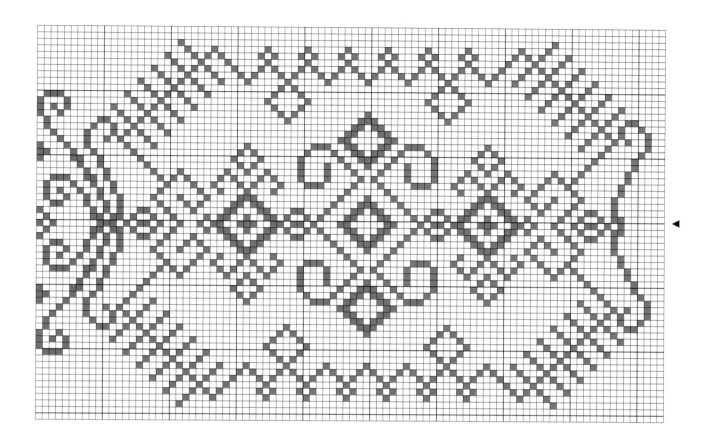

Red and white throw

This white throw with its decorative red embroidery is actually a traditionally patterned tablecloth from former Yugoslavia. With five different motifs used repeatedly all over the cloth, it comprises four identical squares crocheted together to make a larger square. Each square is a large ready-made linen table mat, with perforated edges, each of which has been edged with crochet either to hold the pieces together or to add a fringing.

MATERIALS

For the cross-stitch design:

white linen, 27½in (70cm) square

dark cotton thread

sewing needle

5 skeins of rosy red (DMC 347) stranded cotton

tapestry needle

scissors

SIZE

Each square of the throw measures 27½in (70cm) square. The completed throw measures 110in (280cm) square.

◀ The fringing shown here is in white and red to match the cloth. You could make a similar one by plaiting the threads before fringing.

Making the throw

To make one piece of the throw, baste the central vertical and horizontal lines across the linen square with dark cotton thread to find the center. Then baste another cross in each quarter of the fabric, so that the fabric is divided into eight segments.

Following the chart, begin cross stitching the central flower motif, the center of which will be the center of the linen, using two strands of cotton in the needle. Then work the motifs from the basted lines, which are your guidelines. When you have completed the main motifs you can then embroider the border, with its repeating flowers and loops. Make further pieces of the throw as desired.

▶ This beautiful, antique cross-stitch tablecloth combines many different motifs including geometric and naturalist shapes. It has been used here as a decorative throw to complement the gingham sofa on which it is sitting.

◄ A series of L shapes are joined together down a diagonal line to create a leaf skeleton shape. It is anchored at its base with five alternate crosses forming a square.

▲ This circular motif has arms radiating from its center. The motif in the middle of the circle is like a snowflake in its design and could be used on its own.

▲ A cross-stitch motif of a bird sitting on a branch surrounded by leaves. By changing the angle of the bird's head, the character appears to change from inquiring to malevolent.

▲ This intricate motif features two birds seated on a carnation. Note how much of the pattern is made by variations on a theme, with cross stitches being turned to make diagonals. The figure "92" in the bottom right-hand corner is the year in which it was stitched—1892.

▲ This small square motif is made by radiating Ls from the cross in the center of the pattern.

◄ This motif is similar to the tree of life, which appears in cultures as far apart as India and Switzerland and is common throughout Eastern Europe.

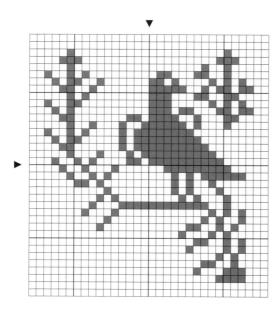

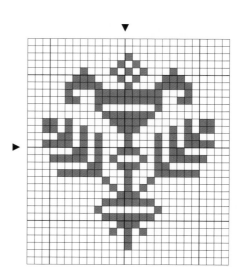

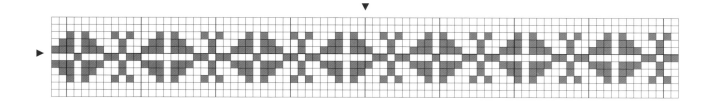

THREAD COLOR

		Anchor	DMC
	Rosy red	13	347

Black and white runner

This beautiful runner is a traditionally patterned Transylvanian piece, dating back to the turn of the century. It was discovered in a tiny antique shop along the back streets of Budapest, hidden away among the blankets, cloths, and sheets.

The fabric is a heavyweight, coarse linen in its natural color. It has been cross stitched using a black woolen yarn and, although the stitches are large, they are also dense so the piece looks like a tapestry.

MATERIALS

For the cross-stitch design:

natural unbleached linen or heavy cotton, 20 x 82in (50 x 205cm)

dark cotton thread

sewing needle

20 skeins of black woolen yarn

tapestry needle

dressmaker's scissors

SIZE

The completed design measures 18 x 78in (46 x 294cm). The actual runner measures 20 x 80in (52 x 200cm).

◄ When cross stitching with wool on a heavyweight coarse linen, the work is liable to become distorted.

Making the runner

The main pattern of the runner consists of two borders, the interlocking triangular shapes and the diamond shapes, which run in alternate rows along the runner. There are three rows of interlocking triangles, and two full rows and two half rows of the diamonds. The border design of the runner is very simple, with shadowed triangular shapes set in between two straight lines.

Before you begin to cross stitch, compare your fabric to the pattern chart and work out the size of your stitches; the one in the photograph has eight stitches per inch or three stitches per centimeter. Using dark cotton thread, baste guidelines across the linen.

Begin cross stitching the design at one end and work down to the other using black yarn. Blanket stitch around all the edges to finish.

► This embroidered runner can be used to decorate any rectangular piece of furniture, from the top of a dresser or console table to an old chest, as shown here.

THREAD COLOR

		Appleton	**DMC**
■	Black tapestry yarn	993	7309

Needle cases

These needle cases are ideal for showing off tiny pieces of cross stitch and will probably appeal to the beginner as they are quick and easy to stitch as well as being handy items for storing needles. In fact, this project will probably require you to spend more time making up the needle case itself than stitching the design, as both parts of the process are very minimal.

MATERIALS

For the cross-stitch design:

11-count, white Aida fabric

embroidery hoop

1 skein of red (DMC 321) stranded cotton

tapestry needle

Other materials:

stiff cardboard, 3¼ x 6½in (8 x 16.5cm)

pencil

ruler

scalpel

red brocade fabric, 3½ x 7in (9 x 17.5cm)

dressmaker's scissors

fabric glue

paintbrush

red and white gingham fabric, 2¾ x 6¼in (7 x 15.5cm)

short length of lace

plastic needle holder

SIZE

The completed design measures 3in (7.5cm) square.

◄ These two needle cases are made from cardboard covered with fabric and embellished with a cross-stitch design. The insides of the cases are lined with homespun fabric in red and white.

► A needle case is a very quick and easy cross-stitch project and can be worked in an evening. This would make an ideal gift for a keen needleperson.

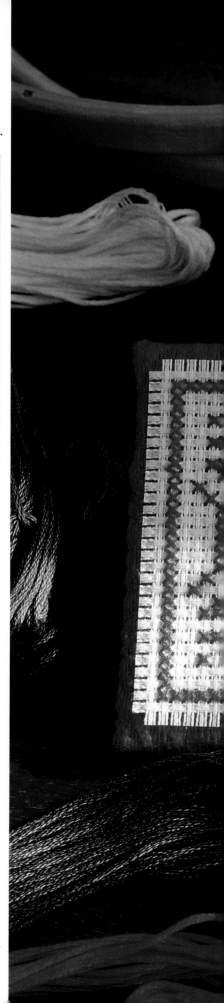

Getting started

Choose from the charted designs a motif you like. Stitch the small cross-stitch motif, using two strands of the six-stranded cotton. Although the final piece will only be a 2½in (6cm) square, you should work on a larger piece of Aida fabric, so that it will fit into an embroidery hoop. When you have completed the cross stitch cut the piece out, leaving three squares of Aida fabric all around. Fray two of these three squares. The cross-stitch piece will now be ready to fit on to the needle case.

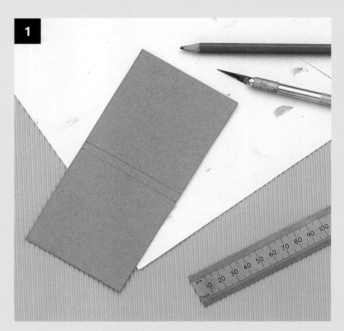

Making up a needle case

1 Mark the center of the cardboard with a pencil and ruler, measuring 3in (8cm) in from each side, leaving a ¼in (5mm) central panel. The cardboard needs to be folded like a book with a spine, so score the lines that you have marked with a scalpel and fold.

2 Place the red brocade fabric, wrong side facing up, on a flat surface. Then lay the cardboard with the penciled lines facing upwards, on top of the fabric, so that the fabric can still be seen all around the edges. Using fabric glue to secure the fabric in place, fold the fabric over all the edges, and glue in position.

3 When the glue has dried, lay the red and white gingham over the cardboard to cover up the raw edges of the brocade. Cut two short lengths of lace and place them underneath the gingham lining on each side of the case, so that they overlap the edges. Glue the lace and lining in place, adding a tiny amount of glue to the inside of the spine for extra security.

4 Glue the plastic needle holder inside the needle case and then glue the cross-stitch piece on to the front cover of the case to finish.

TIP BOX

If you would like to use a finer type of fabric to cover your needle case, test the fabric glue on a scrap of the fabric to see whether it shows through. If it does, you could try using double-sided tape instead of fabric glue.

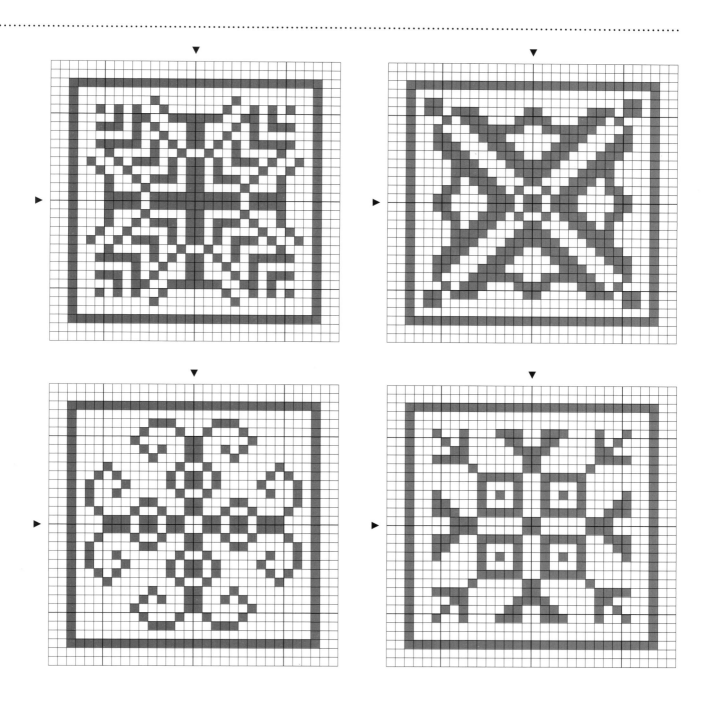

THREAD COLOR

		Anchor	DMC
	Red	47	321

DINING ROOMS

Tablecloths, table mats, and napkins can all be transformed with the addition of decorative cross-stitch motifs and borders to create a stylish touch for a dinner party. You could decorate all your table linen with the same range of motifs, repeating elements from the tablecloth for the corners of each napkin. Alternatively, you could stitch separate motifs on each item of linen, linking them together by color.

A selection of greeting cards is also included in this chapter. Not only are they perfect for giving on birthdays, but they can also be framed as pictures or worked on cushions, napkins, and other linens.

Table mat and napkin

The table mat and matching napkin were made from a beautiful heavyweight linen fabric in a coffee color, and embroidered with bronze and yellow embroidery threads. The motifs bordering the edges of the table mat are little stylized trees; one element was taken from the design and applied to a single corner of the napkin.

The edges of the mat and napkin were frayed to finish. If you prefer, you could hem the edges by hand or machine.

▲ Inspired by autumn colors, this napkin is made from brown linen with a golden tree cross stitched into a corner.

MATERIALS FOR EACH MAT OR NAPKIN

For the cross-stitch design:

brown linen, 30cm (12in) square

tape measure

pins

white cotton thread and sewing needle (optional)

embroidery hoop

1 skein of bronze (DMC 973) stranded cotton

tapestry needle

1 skein of yellow (DMC 782) stranded cotton

scissors

iron

SIZE

The completed design measures 12in (30cm) square.

▶ This napkin and table mat are stitched with the same motif in different but complementary colors. The tree is alternated with a checkerboard of cross-stitched squares all round its border, while the napkin has only the one motif stitched in a single corner.

𝒢etting started

Although I have chosen brown linen for these table mats and napkins, white or cream would look equally as good. If you wish to change the dimension of the mat or napkin, you could add more of the border motif and then insert the corner motif as given in the chart.

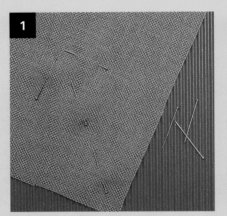

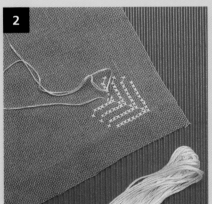

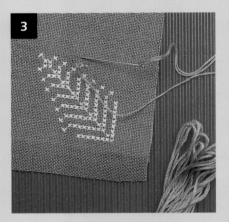

Working the cross stitch

1 From the outside edges of the linen square, measure in 1½in (4cm) and mark the points with pins. If you like, you could stitch basting stitches in white cotton along all the edges of the square, using the pins as guides.

2 Place the linen in the hoop and, starting from the basted or pinned line, begin cross stitching in toward the center, using two strands of stranded cotton. Follow the chart for either the table mat or the napkin, and use the yellow cotton first. As the linen is quite fine, do not make your cross stitches too small; they should be about ⅛in (3mm) in size, and you should be stitching about 7 to 9 stitches per 1in (2.5cm).

3 When you have completed all the stitching in the first color, complete the design using the bronze stranded embroidery cotton.

Finishing the mat

4 Remove the linen from the hoop and press it flat with a hot iron. Then carefully begin to fray the edges of the linen by pulling out four or five strands of linen at each edge. Trim the frayed edges to neaten, if you feel it necessary.

Table mat chart

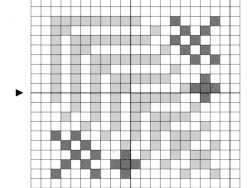

Table napkin chart

THREAD COLORS

		Anchor	DMC
	Bronze	297	973
	Yellow	307	782

Bordered tablecloth

This huge tablecloth made from beautiful white linen was decorated with a cross-stitched border in soft blue silk, running along the entire length and breadth of the cloth. It was purchased from an antique shop in Budapest and is believed to be over 100 years old. The fact that the tablecloth is in the most perfect condition with no sign of wear says something about the durability of linen; if it is looked after properly, it can last for many years.

MATERIALS

For the cross-stitch design:

linen tablecloth

dark cotton thread

sewing needle

denim blue (DMC 311) stranded cotton (the number of skeins depends on the size of your tablecloth—6 skeins is enough for 31in (80cm) of this border)

tapestry needle

embroidery hoop

scissors

SIZE

The width of the design measures 3in (8cm).

◄ This simple vine leaf design set between castellated borders is worked in mid-blue.

Making the tablecloth
The tablecloth measures 49 x 119in (125 x 304cm). The border is the only part of the cloth decorated with cross stitching, and it runs along all the edges. The motifs are plain, but over such a length they look stunning. To make a tablecloth like this, it is best to buy a ready-made tablecloth the size you require; ensure that it is a good quality heavyweight linen.

Use dark cotton thread to baste guidelines along the borders of the tablecloth where you will be stitching. Then, following the chart, stitch the design using two strands of denim blue stranded cotton. First stitch two opposite borders along the length of the cloth. Then work the remaining two sides along the width of the tablecloth, except where the first two borders cross.

▶ The cross-stitched border of this tablecloth does not go round the corner but works rather like a tram line, with one border crossing the adjacent one. This makes the design easy to scale up or down to make a larger or smaller cloth.

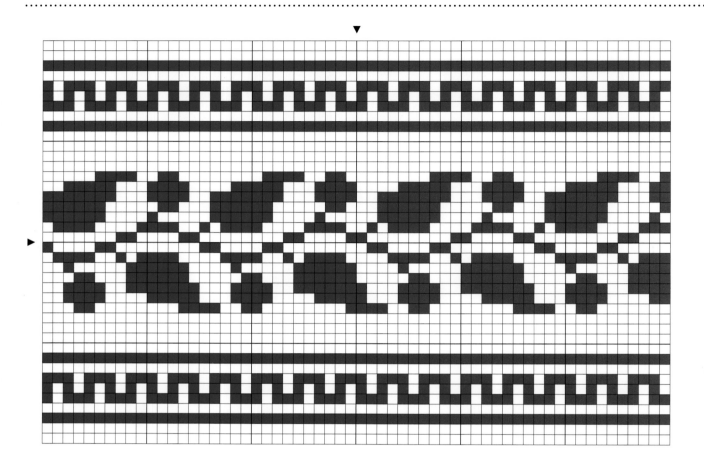

THREAD COLOR

		Anchor	DMC
	Denim blue	148	311

Red and blue tablecloth

The tablecloth pictured here and on page 10 is an old one I borrowed from a friend whose grandmother made it. It actually consists of 15 small squares, stitched together in three rows of five squares to form a rectangular-shaped cloth. The edges of each individual square have been turned under and blanket stitched; the loops of the blanket stitches have been picked up and used to sew the squares together with red embroidery thread.

Making the tablecloth
To make a tablecloth similar to this you will need to cut out 15 pieces of heavy white cotton fabric, each measuring 12½in (32cm) square; this includes a ¼in (6mm) allowance around each edge for the blanket-stitched hems.

Before stitching the motifs, baste guidelines with dark cotton thread through the center of the motifs. The diamond motif is in fact the square motif rotated through 90 degrees. Plot a simple chart based on this

design. Stitch the motifs using two strands of embroidery cotton in the needle.

When you have completed cross stitching each motif, turn under each edge of the squares and blanket stitch around the edges with the light blue embroidery cotton. Then stitch each piece together with red embroidery thread, catching the loops on each blanket stitch with the needle. To finish the tablecloth, you may add a fringe around the edges if desired.

◄ This detail of the tablecloth shows the red and blue design worked both as a square and then turned 90 degrees and worked as a diamond. The squares of the tablecloth are edged in blanket stitch and then sewn as patchwork.

Greetings cards

The inspiration behind these unusual greeting card designs came from some wonderful mosaics of zodiac signs I saw in a swimming pool when I was on holiday in Minorca. In fact, most mosaics can easily be adapted into cross-stitch designs as they are often worked on a grid in the same way as counted needlework designs. The designs are quick and simple to stitch and make ideal birthday cards for friends and relatives throughout the year.

MATERIALS

For the cross-stitch design:

14-count, light blue Aida

dark cotton thread

sewing needle

embroidery hoop

1 skein of dark blue (DMC 820) stranded cotton

1 skein of white (DMC blanc) stranded cotton

Other materials:

pencil

fabric glue

paintbrush

scissors

blank greeting cards

SIZE

Each design measures approximately 2¼in (6cm) square.

▼ This design depicts Capricorn, the goat. It is set in a dark blue card with a ready-cut circular mount, the shape of which suits the scale and size of the image.

▲ This design shows the star sign of Sagittarius worked in dark blue on a light blue Aida fabric.

▶ Two fish, symbols of Pisces, are here shown swimming round and round their circular goldfish bowl mount.

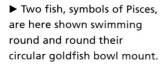

▶ Cross-stitch greetings cards can be more than simply cards, they can become keepsakes. These cross-stitch designs featuring signs of the zodiac may be used to decorate napkins or paperweights as well as birthday cards.

Getting started

These greeting cards are great for beginners to stitch. Being small, they are a good way of using up remnants of thread and Aida fabric. Although I have kept to a sea-blue theme the designs would look equally good on a cream or white background. You can also vary the color of the blank greeting cards to echo or contrast with the thread color. The same motifs could also be stitched on a paperweight or pillowcase.

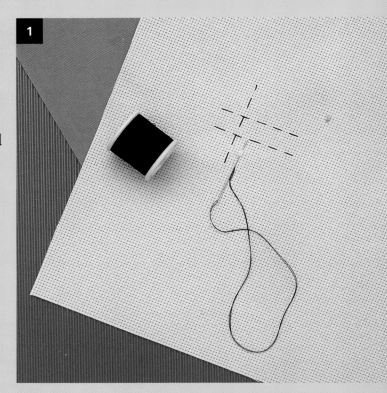

Working the cross stitch

1 Work out the number of stitches and the central lines of the motif you are going to work on; the Capricorn sign of the goat is featured in this project. Using dark-colored cotton thread, baste the central vertical and horizontal lines on the Aida fabric.

2 Following the chart, work the cross stitching using two strands of the main color of stranded cotton first, in this case dark blue. First stitch the outlines, then fill in the body.

3 When you have completed stitching the first color, go on to stitch the hooves, eyes, and horns of the goat using two strands of white stranded embroidery cotton.

Making up the card

4 When you have completed the cross stitching, mark off a rectangle around the stitched motif in pencil that is slightly larger than the hole in the blank greeting card. The pencil will not be visible when the card is completed. Trim the Aida fabric along the marked lines with a pair of scissors.

5 Finally, brush a small amount of fabric glue all around the right side edges of the Aida, then carefully place it in position on the blank greeting card so that the motif is clearly visible through the aperture in the card. Close up the greeting card, press it in between a couple of hardback books so that it dries flat, and allow to dry for half an hour.

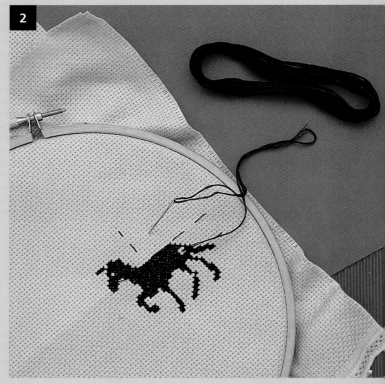

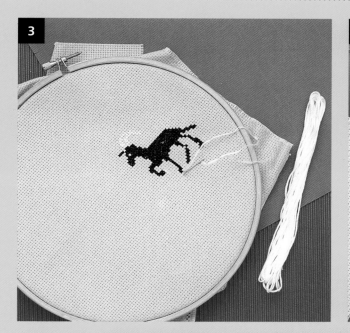

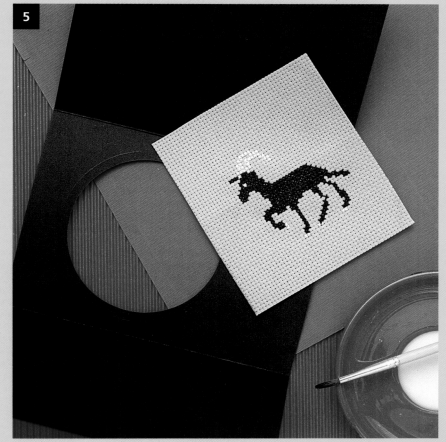

TIP BOX

When working at this scale it is easy to make the stitching too thick and the tension too tight. It is a good idea to stitch a practice piece before beginning your actual design, trying it with one, two, and three strands of thread in the needle, to see which one works best. These designs were stitched with two strands.

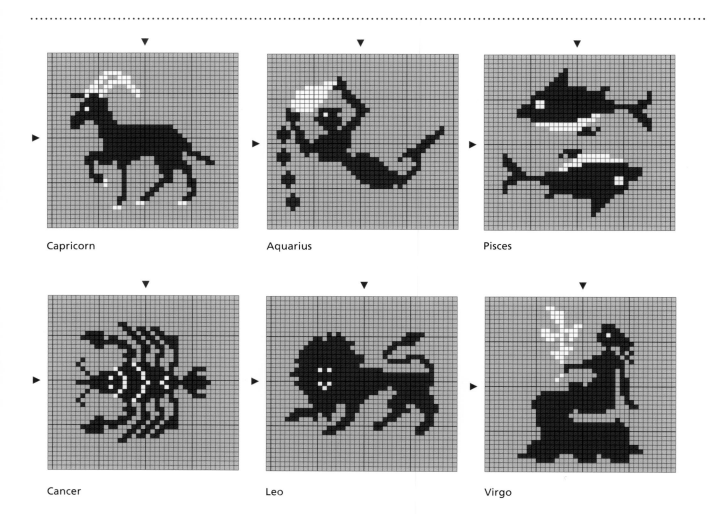

Capricorn

Aquarius

Pisces

Cancer

Leo

Virgo

THREAD COLORS

		Anchor	**DMC**
■	Dark blue	134	820
□	White	White	Blanc

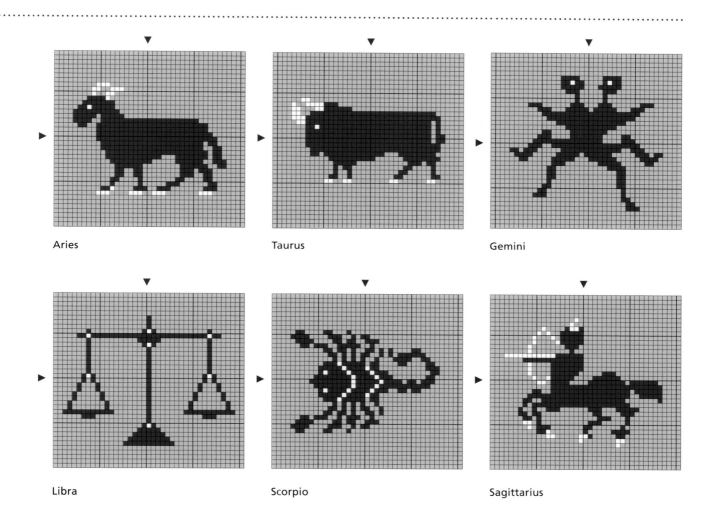

Aries

Taurus

Gemini

Libra

Scorpio

Sagittarius

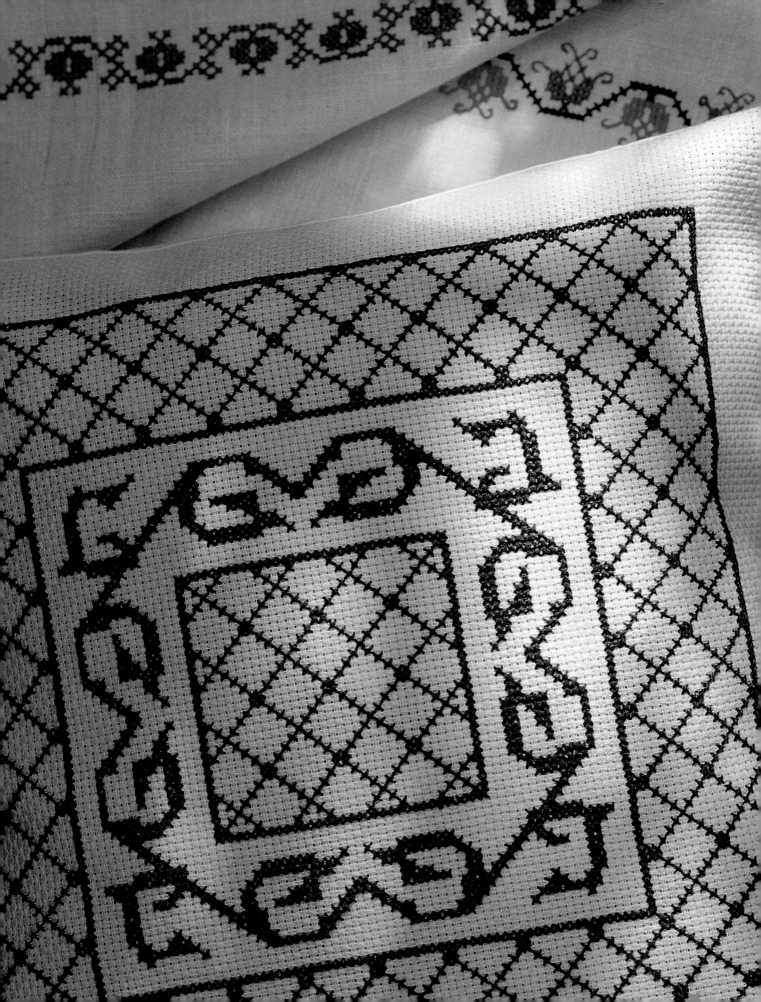

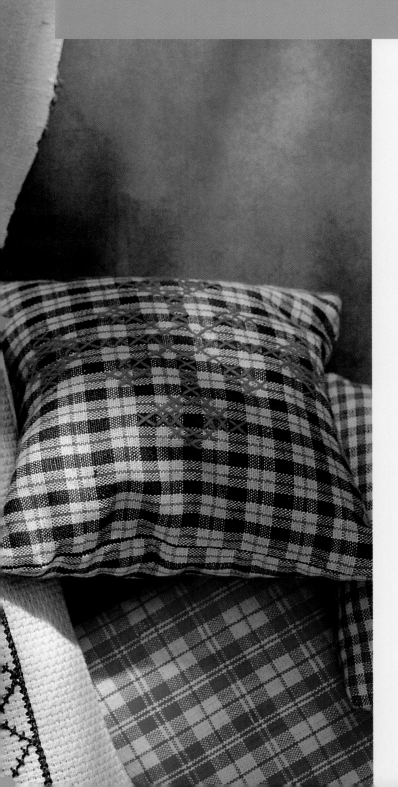

BEDROOMS

$\mathcal{E}$veryday items, such as cushion covers and bed linen, can be given a real lift with a few simple yet well-placed cross-stitch motifs and designs. Transform a tired old cushion with a single primary color and a bold geometric pattern, or stitch a few tiny lavender cushions to place in lingerie drawers or arrange among bedding. You could personalize pillowcases to make elegant gifts for yourself or for loved ones, or create your own cross-stitch frames to provide attractive and interesting borders for your old photographs and holiday postcards.

Photograph frame

This beautiful cross-stitch frame is inspired by Scandinavian embroidery motifs and makes an ideal border for sepia photographs for the dressing table. The half-flower design used for the body of the frame is a very popular Norwegian motif and can also be found in Finnish work. Simple and versatile, this design, like many other cross-stitch designs, can be used in beadwork and knitting as well as cross-stitch work.

MATERIALS

For the cross-stitch design:

14-count, cream Aida fabric

contrasting basting thread

sewing needle

embroidery hoop

2 skeins of red (DMC 304) stranded cotton

tapestry needle

Other materials:

iron

scissors

mat knife

ruler

cardboard

fabric glue

pins

SIZE

The completed frame measures 8½in (21.5cm) square with an internal edge of 4in (10cm).

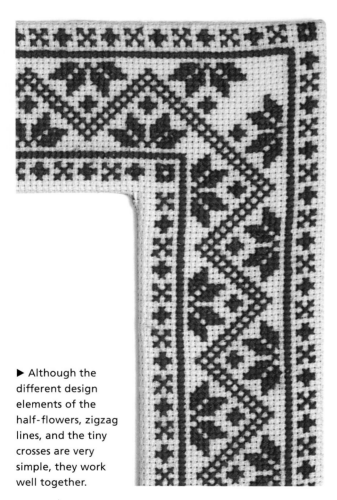

▶ Although the different design elements of the half-flowers, zigzag lines, and the tiny crosses are very simple, they work well together.

▶ Set among old, silver-framed family pictures on a dressing table, this charming cross-stitched frame comes into its own as a border for a favorite photograph.

Getting started

Frames are most easily worked as a rectangle of cloth which is then cut into a frame shape and mounted on to cardboard once the stitching has been completed. By following step 1 and working out exactly where to place the stitching, a neat and symmetrical frame will be achieved. Always allow at least 3-4in (7.5-10cm) around the Aida fabric to pull over the frame base.

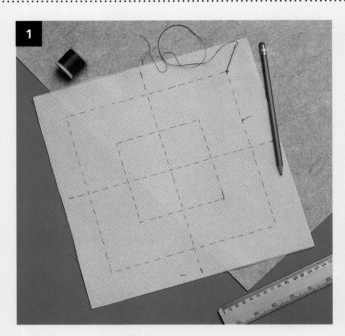

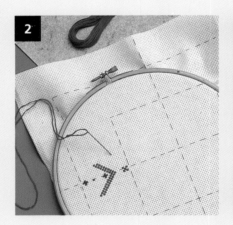

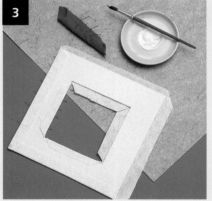

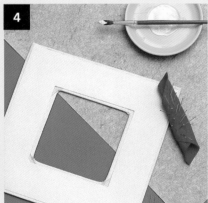

Working the cross stitch

1 When you have decided on the size of your frame, mark the center of the design on the fabric. To do this, fold the fabric in half and then in half again and baste along the folds created. Then mark the inner and outer edges of the frame with basting stitches.

2 Place the fabric in an embroidery hoop and, starting at the center of one of the long sides of the frame and following the chart, begin cross stitching the design using three strands of stranded cotton in the needle. Move the fabric along in the hoop as you work each area of the design, keeping it taut as you stitch. When the design is finished, remove the fabric from the hoop and press the wrong side of the embroidery using a warm iron, ironing quickly so as not to scorch the Aida fabric.

Making up the frame

3 Cut out the fabric frame leaving a ½in (12mm) border on both the inside and the outside of the frame. Using a mat knife, cut a piece of cardboard the same dimensions as the cross-stitch frame. Miter all the corners of the fabric frame and then glue and pin the corners on to the cardboard.

4 Remove the pins and back the frame with cardboard.

TIP BOX

If the cross-stitch work distorts as you work, dampen it with a spray of water then stretch and manipulate it into shape across the cardboard base of the photograph frame.

THREAD COLOR

		Anchor	DMC
▬	Dark red	760	304

Monogrammed pillowcases

These two luxurious Egyptian cotton Oxford pillowcases have been cross stitched with initials in fresh denim blue embroidery cotton as a gift. The color of the embroidery allows the pillows to be placed in a variety of color schemes, from light blues to vivid reds and oranges. To monogram your pillowcases, pick out your chosen initials from the alphabet charts (see pages 108–11), then add tiny motifs in between the letters to tie them together and to add a delicate finishing touch. Here we have used tiny diamond shapes.

MATERIALS

For the cross-stitch design:

pillowcase

tape measure

embroidery hoop

1 skein of light denim blue (DMC 798) stranded cotton

tapestry needle

waste canvas (optional)

scissors

pins

SIZE

The completed design measures 8 x 2in (20 x 5cm).

Decorating the pillowcase

To monogram your pillowcase, first find the center. Measure from the top right-hand corner to the bottom left-hand corner, and mark the center with pins. Then measure from the top left-hand corner to the bottom right-hand corner; the center should coincide with the first mark made. If you are stitching three initials, this center point will be the center of the middle letter.

Place the pillowcase in an embroidery hoop, remembering to allow only one thickness of fabric through the hoop, so as not to sew the two sides of the pillowcase together. Starting at the central point of the middle letter, and using two strands of the stranded cotton, begin to cross stitch the letter. If the cotton is very fine it will be difficult to use the weave of the fabric as a guide. Try to stitch approximately 12 stitches per inch (5 stitches per centimeter). This is very fine work, but the type of fabric you are using dictates the size of the stitches; if you use a much looser woven fabric like linen, the stitches will be larger.

If you are not comfortable working in this manner, baste a piece of fine waste canvas to the pillowcase. Work the cross stitch through both the waste canvas and the pillowcase, then carefully pull out the threads of the waste canvas one by one when the cross stitching is complete.

When you have completed stitching the middle of the three initials, measure ⅝in (1.5cm) from the center of each side of the letter, and stitch in the tiny diamond shapes. Then measure the same distance again from the diamond shapes on each side and stitch the first and last initials, ensuring that they are the same height and width as the central initial.

▶ Lovely as gifts, keepsakes, or for the trousseau drawer, monogrammed pillowcases are always treasured and often passed on down through the family.

Linen hand towels

These old-fashioned linen hand towels originated in Hungary and are possibly up to 100 years old, yet they still look as fresh and inviting as they did when they were first made. They are beautiful examples of simple borders worked on wonderful fabric. The simplicity and the beauty of both the workmanship and the linen fabric make them sought after and well loved. Linen is a good fabric for hand towels, being very absorbent and easy to wash, looking fresh and new after each wash. The cross-stitch patterns given have been slightly altered and the non-cross-stitch elements removed. Your final piece will be like that given on the chart, while still very similar to the towels pictured.

MATERIALS

For the cross-stitch design:

off-white linen, 38 x 20in (95 x 50cm)

tape measure

dark cotton thread

2 skeins of blue (DMC 517) stranded cotton

tapestry needle

1 skein of dark green (DMC 500) stranded cotton

1 skein of light blue (DMC 799) stranded cotton

1 skein of red (DMC 321) stranded cotton

Other materials:

white sewing thread

sewing needle

iron

scissors

SIZE

The border width on the completed design measures 1in (2.5cm).

Decorating the towels

These embroidered towels are made from heavy off-white linen. The two shorter ends are hemmed finely and the two longer sides are actually the selvage edges of the linen. If you cannot obtain linen with a narrow width and cannot get the selvage edges on either side, just cut a larger piece of linen and hem it all around the edges with strong thread and invisible slip stitches before you begin the cross stitching.

From the shorter edges, measure up 4-4¾in (10-12cm) and baste a line of dark cotton thread stitches parallel to the shorter edge on both sides of the linen, keeping the line straight and even.

To stitch the towel with the single blue border, use two strands of blue stranded cotton in the needle. To stitch the border of the other towel, you will need one strand of stranded cotton of each color in the needle. Use the basted line as a guide for the bottom of the border. Work about 10 stitches an inch (4 stitches a centimeter) working in one color first, completing the work in that color, and then moving on to the next. When you have completed the cross-stitch pattern, carefully remove the basting stitches and press the towel flat.

▶ Old-fashioned cross-stitched linen towels add a touch of nostalgia and hint of the country to any bedroom.

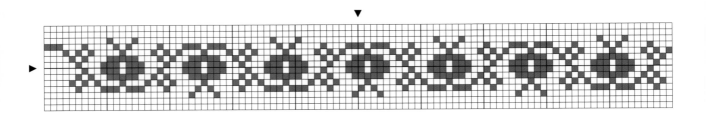

◀ This simple cross-stitched border depicts a row of roses and leaves. The chart shows a slightly altered version, with the flower protruding over the outer edge of the border.

THREAD COLORS

		Anchor	DMC
	Blue	170	517
	Dark green	879	500
	Light blue	130	799
	Red	47	321

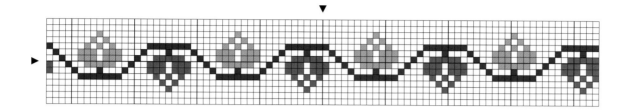

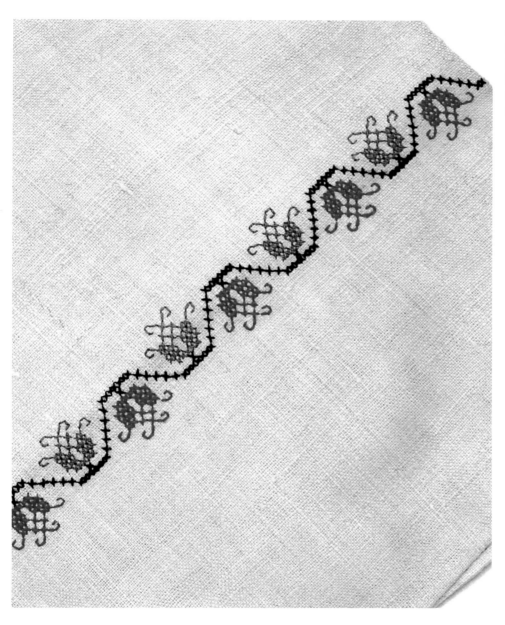

◄ The original stitched-border design features backstitch decoration, which has been removed from the chart to produce more stylized flowers and stems.

Celtic trellis cushion

The inspiration for this cross-stitch cushion was a trellis and Celtic motifs, which were stylized and intertwined to create the square design. As the design is strong and geometric, it looks stylish in just one color. The same trellis pattern could be used equally effectively with a rosebud motif in place of the Celtic motifs, and using green thread in place of blue. Aida fabric, the easiest fabric to work cross stitch on with its equal and symmetrical weave, was used as the background fabric.

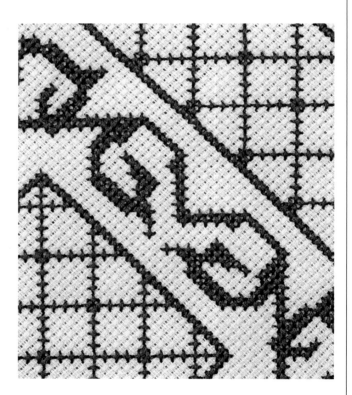

▲ This detail of the cushion shows how the simple Celtic cross-stitch pattern frames the decorative inner trellis border.

▶ This cross-stitched cushion coordinates beautifully with the seat cover of the chair. Choose the color of cotton to match your decor.

MATERIALS

For the cross-stitch design:

pencil

ruler

graph paper, 11 squares to 1in (2.5cm)

colored pencils (optional)

11-count, cream Aida fabric, 12in (30cm) square

contrasting basting thread

sewing needle

scissors

embroidery hoop

3 skeins of blue (DMC 825) stranded cotton

tapestry needle

Other materials:

iron

20in (0.5m) fabric for cushion cover backing

pins

matching sewing thread

sewing machine

cushion pad, 12½in (32cm) square

SIZE

The completed design measures 9¾in (25cm) square. The completed cushion measures 12½in (32cm) square.

Getting started

This is a fairly intricate pattern and takes concentration. As it is worked in one color there are no easy ways of separating one part of the pattern from another. You might find it helpful to put a pencil line through each line of the paper pattern when you have finished stitching it.

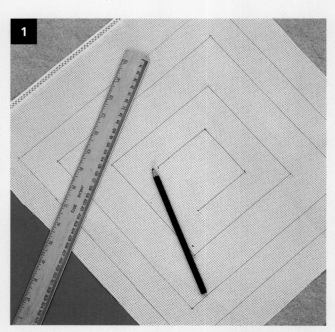

Working the cross stitch

1 Using a pencil and ruler, draw the cushion design on to graph paper or copy the design shown. One square represents one cross stitch. If you decide to use more than one color, go over the pencil lines with colored pencils to indicate what color is to be used where. Mark the center of the design.

2 Copying the paper design, draw the outside and inside of the trellis on Aida fabric. Draw diagonal lines across the design to mark the center. Go over the lines with large basting stitches in a contrasting color. Turn the canvas over so that you can follow the basting lines, without the pencil lines showing on the finished piece of work.

3 Stretch the canvas taut in an embroidery hoop. Starting at the center of the fabric and following the chart or your penciled design, cross stitch the design using two strands of blue stranded cotton in the needle. Move the fabric in the hoop as you work each area of the design.

Making up the cushion

4 When the design is finished, remove it from the hoop and press it flat on the reverse side. The finished design should be the size of the cushion pad plus 1¼in (3cm) all around for a seam allowance. To make the back of the cushion, cut two pieces of fabric measuring 12¾ x 9in (32 x 22.5cm). Hem both pieces of fabric along one long end. Pin and baste the two back pieces of fabric so that the hemmed ends overlap and together make the same size as the cushion front. With right sides together, machine the cross-stitched cushion front to the envelope back. To prevent fraying, stitch around the edges with a machine zigzag stitch. Insert the cushion pad through the back flap to finish.

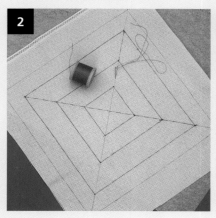

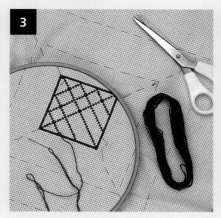

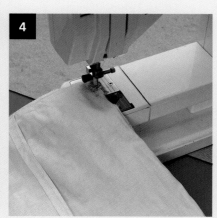

THREAD COLOR

		Anchor	DMC
▬	Blue	162	825

Drawstring bags

These simple drawstring bags can be used as wash bags or pouches for storing herbs, dried flowers, or potpourri. For best results, use plain fabrics such as gingham, calico, and hessian; the embroidery would not show up well against highly patterned fabrics. The cross-stitch designs are taken from traditional English samplers—a tree of life, doves, and sheep, each intertwined with initials—and, being limited to three shades of blue, are very easy to complete.

MATERIALS

For the cross-stitch design:

14-count, antique white Aida fabric

contrasting basting thread

sewing needle

embroidery hoop

2 skeins each of blue (DMC shades 995, 336, 312, and 807) stranded cotton

tapestry needle

Other materials:

iron

gingham fabric (the amount will depend on the size of bag you wish to make)

scissors

ruler

pins

matching sewing thread

sewing machine

safety pin

SIZE

The sheep and doves designs each measure 6½ x 9½in (16.5 x 24cm); the tree of life design measures 7¼ x 10in (18.5 x 25.5cm)

▼ This eye-catching motif of a bird of paradise with its vibrant wings and beak is frequently used to flank intertwined initials.

▲ This classic ram motif is a strong and effective shape in embroidery, which becomes more interesting the closer one looks at it.

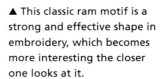

▶ A selection of embroidered drawstring bags stuffed with potpourri makes a pretty and fragrant display hanging on an antique pegboard.

Getting started

Each cross-stitch design for the drawstring bags incorporates a pair of scriptlike initials. If you wish to personalize your design—to create a birthday gift for a special friend, for example—substitute your chosen initials for those featured in the charts. If you are making all three drawstring bags, work the cross stitch on one piece of Aida to save fabric, ensuring that you leave enough of a border for cutting and turning between each design.

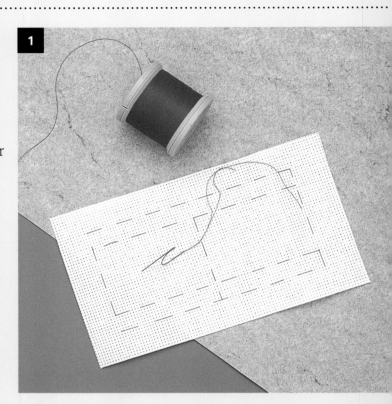

Working the cross stitch

1 Referring to the charts on page 68, choose the design you wish to work. Mark the center of the Aida fabric with large basting stitches and fix it into an embroidery hoop to keep it taut. Move the fabric along as you work each area. Starting at the center of the fabric and following the chart, work the design in cross stitch using three strands of stranded embroidery cotton in the needle. When the cross-stitch design is complete, remove the Aida fabric from the hoop and press the embroidery on the reverse side with a warm iron. Fold the raw edges under neatly.

Constructing the bag

2 Using a pair of sharp scissors, carefully cut two rectangles, each measuring 6¾ x 12¼in (17 x 32cm), from the gingham fabric; these will make the main body of the bag. Then cut two strips measuring 15¾ x 2in (40 x 5cm) for the two drawstrings. From one short end of each rectangle, measure down 3in (8cm), fold the material then press across this fold with a hot iron.

3 Take one of the rectangles of gingham fabric and, making sure that the fold of material made in step 2 is facing away from you, pin the cross-stitched piece 2in (5cm) from the base of the fabric. Sew the design in place around each side by hand, making sure that all stitching is carefully concealed.

4 With right sides facing, pin the two rectangular pieces of gingham together around three sides. Leaving the folded edges open, sew around the other three sides—start sewing just after the turnover on one side and stop short of the turnover on the final side.

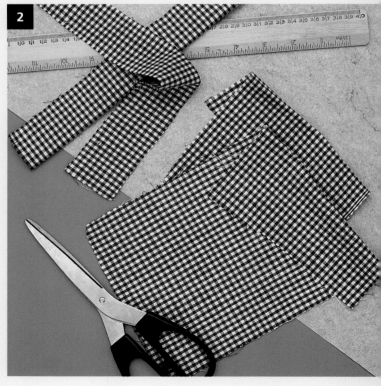

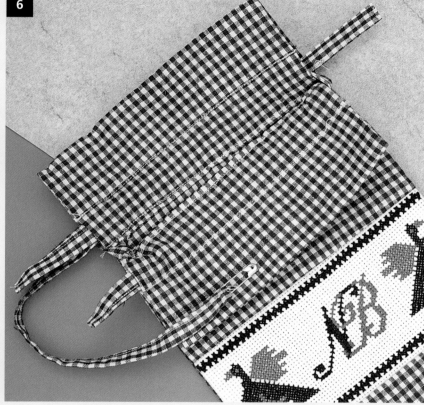

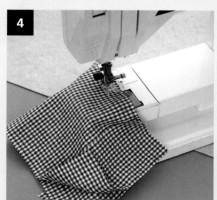

5 To make a channel for the drawstring, turn under the raw edge of the first fold and sew it in place, close to the edge and right across the width of the bag. From this point, move up 1in (2.5cm) and sew another line parallel to the previous row of stitches to make a channel in between them for the drawstring to go through. Repeat the process for the second fold.

6 Fold the gingham strips in half lengthways. Turn in the raw edges and press with a hot iron. Sew them down inside the neat edge, using tiny slip stitches. Then turn them under at the short ends. Attach a safety pin to the end of the first strip and feed this strip through the first channel, around the opening between the channels and out through the second channel.

Remove the safety pin and knot the two loose ends of the gingham strip together. Repeat the process with the other strip but this time feed it in from the opposite end of the bag. Again, knot the two loose ends together, pulling the knot very tightly and as close to the ends as possible. This is to prevent the drawstrings working their way out of the stitched channels. To close the bag, pull the two drawstrings away from each other.

THREAD COLORS

	Anchor	DMC
TREE OF LIFE CHART		
Medium blue	860	312
Light blue	920	807
Sky blue	810	995
SHEEP CHART		
Medium blue	860	312
Light blue	920	807
DOVES CHART		
Navy blue	780	336
Sky blue	810	995

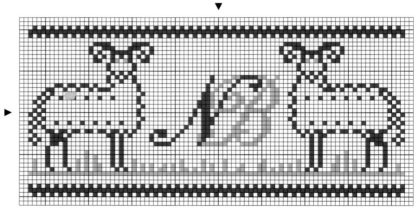

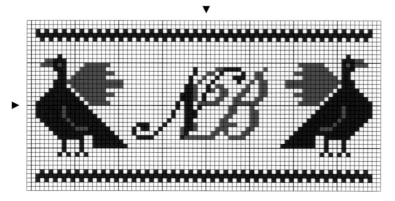

Soap bags

These charming drawstring bags with their stitched daisy motifs, which are also pictured on page 74, provide a delightful way to store your bathroom soaps. For a Shaker look, make them with plain fabrics such as gingham, calico, or even hessian. As they are so easy to make and decorate, you could produce several and hang them from the mirror or arrange them on a shelf for a pretty decoration. You could also use these soap bags as traveling bags and pouches.

Making a soap bag

As these small bags are worked on gingham it is very easy to see just where each individual stitch should be placed. If you wish to line the bags with plastic fabric it is best to do this after the cross stitch has been worked.

To make a bag, fold the main piece of fabric in half lengthways, and sew down the two long edges. Fold down the top open edges by 2in (5cm) and press with a hot iron. Stitch two parallel lines across the fold to make a channel for the

drawstring to go through. Fold the gingham strip in half lengthways and turn in the raw edges, press, and sew down along the fold. Cut the drawstring in half; feed one half through one channel and the second half through the other channel. Knot the ends.

Turn the bag the right way round and, using one gingham square as one stitch, cross stitch a simple design like the one below on to the center front of the bag using two strands of embroidery cotton.

◀ This simple daisy motif is quickly stitched to provide a charming decoration for a soap bag.

*L*avender cushions

For a pretty decoration, and one with a soothing scent, these lavender cushions are a simple, yet effective way, in which to display your talents as a cross stitcher. Working on fabrics other than Aida can make stitching a little bit harder, as you do not have such a definite guide for each stitch. The weave in the fabric has to be your guide, or in this case, gingham fabric checks can guide the direction and size of your stitches.

MATERIALS

For the cross-stitch design:

gingham fabric, 12¾ x 7¼in (32 x 18cm)

embroidery hoop

1 skein of dark blue or red (DMC 823 or 666) stranded cotton

tapestry needle

Other materials:

pencil

ruler

dressmaker's scissors

iron

sewing needle

cotton thread

pins

sewing machine (optional)

lavender

SIZE

The completed dark blue design measures 3 x 2¾in (8 x 7cm). The completed red design measures 3 x 3¾in (10 x 8cm).

◄ Use offcuts of gingham and any color of thread to make these little cushions.

► Charming, decorative and sweetly scented, a lavender cushion is an ideal quick and easy project for a novice cross stitcher to make.

Getting started

When using gingham as a fabric on which to cross stitch, each gingham rectangle equals one cross-stitch square. As gingham is not usually completely symmetrical, however, it means that the finished stitching will not look exactly the same as the pattern on the chart; depending on which way you work on the gingham, your motif will be either wider or larger than the chart motif.

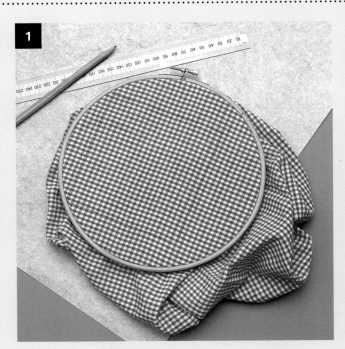

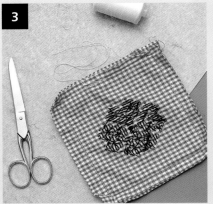

Working the cross stitch

1 Using a pencil and ruler, mark two identical squares, measuring 5½in (14cm), on the gingham fabric. Place the fabric in an embroidery hoop so that one of the squares is centered in the hoop.

2 Following the chart, begin to cross stitch your motif in the center of one of the squares using two strands of stranded cotton in the needle. Use the gingham checks as a guide, and stitch approximately four cross stitches to each check. Complete the design, keeping the stitches the same size.

Making up the cushion

3 Remove the fabric from the embroidery hoop and press it flat with a hot iron. Cut out the two penciled squares with a pair of dressmaker's scissors.

Place the squares right sides together, so that the embroidery is facing inwards, then pin and sew around three and a half sides, either by hand or by machine.

4 Turn the cushion the right way out through the gap and carefully stuff the lavender heads through the opening. Then sew up the opening with tiny over-stitches.

TIP BOX

Fill these stitched lavender bags with other types of potpourri, as desired. There are many different mixes available, and the perfume can always be strengthened with a few drops of scented oil every few months.

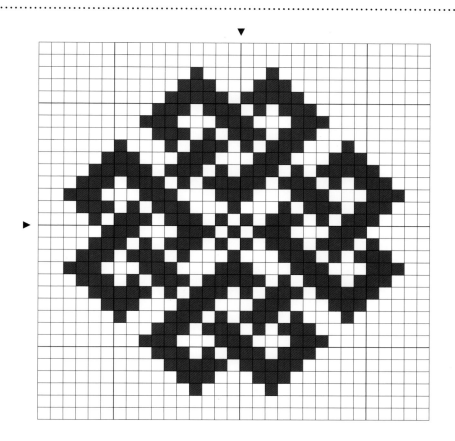

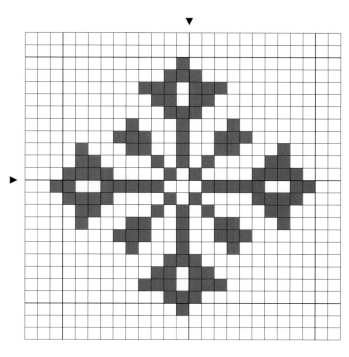

THREAD COLORS

		Anchor	DMC
▪	Dark blue	150	823
▪	Red	46	666

BATHROOMS

The bathroom is often the last room in the house where one thinks of arranging pretty accessories, with the result that it tends to contain a mishmash of uncoordinated bits and pieces. However, even the plainest everyday items can be transformed into elegant objects with a little cross stitching.

Plain white terry towels can be embellished with an embroidered edging, while a laundry bag can be uplifted from its lowly state with a colorful cross-stitch motif on the front.

$\mathscr{E}$mbroidered towels

A simple, yet wonderfully effective way of transforming plain white towels into luxurious accessories is to add cross-stitched strips to the cotton sections at each end. The embroidery was stitched on Aida border strips and then sewn on to the towels. With red cotton on white and white cotton on red, the effect looks fresh and eye-catching. Depending on your level of confidence and cross-stitch skills, the strips can be embroidered with the easy Greek key symbols, or the more advanced trellis pattern.

MATERIALS

For the cross-stitch designs:

dark-colored cotton

sewing needle

5cm (2in) wide red Aida band, long enough to fit along the towel edge

16-count, plain white Aida strip, long enough to fit along the towel edge

embroidery hoop

6 skeins of white (DMC blanc) embroidery cotton

4 skeins of red (DMC 321) embroidery cotton

tapestry needle

Other materials:

white cotton thread

white towels

scissors

pins

iron

SIZE

The completed towel borders measure 2¼in (5.5cm) wide.

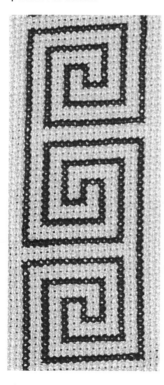

▼ A classic running border motif, the Greek key is a popular, timeless, and simple pattern to stitch.

▲ A little more complicated, this repeating trellis pattern is suitable for the more advanced cross stitcher.

▶ Plain shop-bought towels can be made to look stylish and unique with these cross-stitched bands.

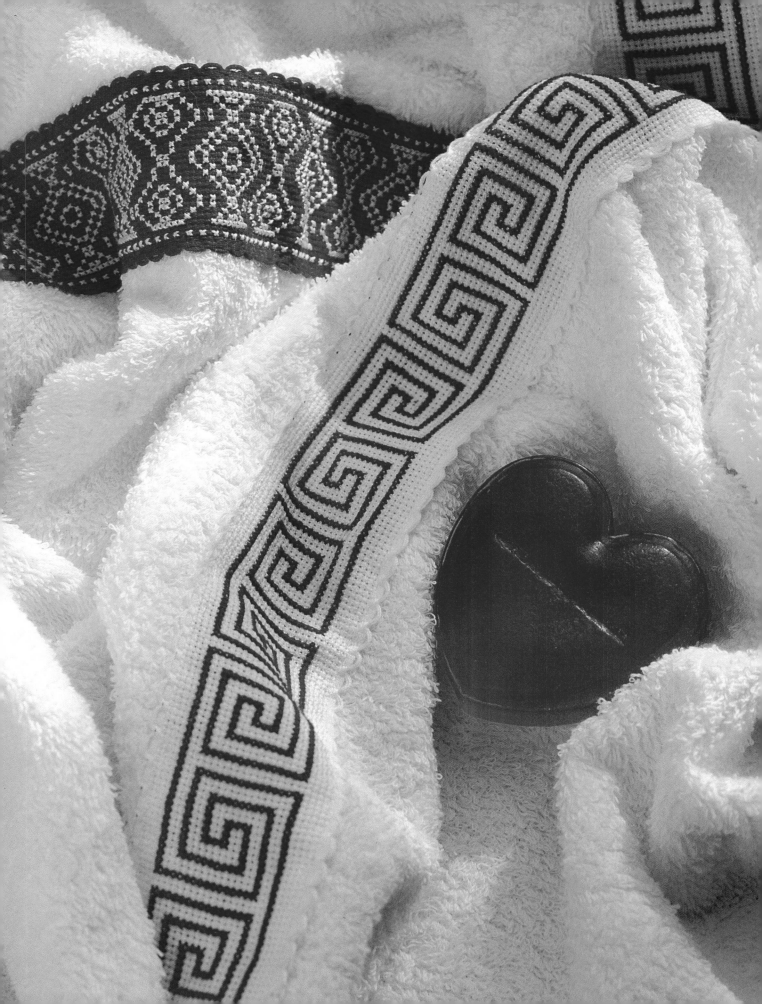

Getting started

As with all cross stitch, the density of the design will be reflected in the number of skeins of embroidery cotton used. When you have completed the initial basting, place the band in the embroidery hoop and tighten. The hoop will be inclined to slacken with the tension only being applied at the two ends rather than all around.

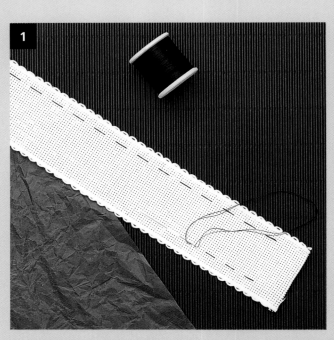

Working the cross stitch

1 Referring to the chart of the repeating Greek key symbol shown opposite, work out the upper and lower edges of the design. Using dark cotton and a needle, baste two lines along the Aida strip as guidelines for the edges of the cross stitching. Then baste the position of the seam allowance for the edge of the towel as a guideline.

2 Starting at one edge of the Aida band, and following the chart, begin cross stitching the design using two strands of embroidery cotton in the needle. You may find it easier to stitch the first half of all the cross stitches for each main motif first.

3 Once you have completed a whole motif in half cross stitch, turn around and go back, completing each half cross stitch with the top half of the cross. In this way, all your cross stitches will lie in the same direction. Continue to stitch the design along the entire length of Aida band until you reach the seam allowance. Make a second cross-stitched strip in the same way if desired.

Completing the towel

4 Carefully pin each embroidered strip into position on the cotton section of the towel (there is one at each end of a towel), ensuring that it is straight. Sew the strip in place using tiny over-stitches around all four edges in a matching thread. Repeat to sew the second strip in place. Then press flat with a warm iron.

> **TIP BOX**
>
> To ensure all the crosses go in the same direction, you may find it easier to stitch half the crosses of the motifs first and then return to stitch the second half of the cross stitches.

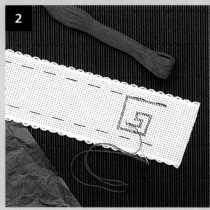

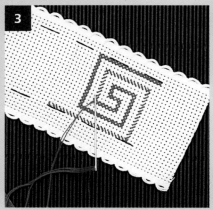

Trellis pattern chart

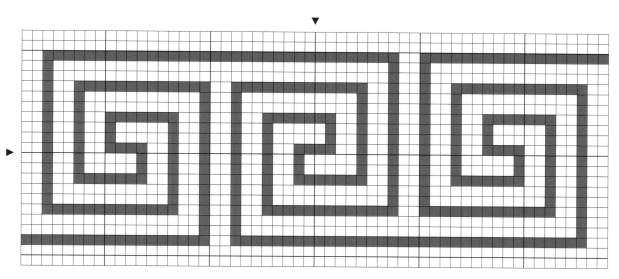

Greek key chart

THREAD COLORS

		Anchor	DMC
☐	White	White	Blanc
▨	Red	9046	321

Towel and linen sash

This decorative and practical sash is similar to those used in many Eastern European countries to tie together freshly washed linens and towels before storing them away. The pattern on the sash is inspired by old cross-stitched designs.

Made from a long strip of linen and cotton binding, the band provides perfect practice for the novice cross stitcher who feels as though he or she can move on from using Aida fabric. The pattern is relatively simple and the fabric has a large weave.

MATERIALS

For the cross-stitch design:

dark-colored thread

sewing needle

off-white linen, 6 x 56in (15 x 142cm)

2 skeins of red (DMC 321) embroidery cotton

tapestry needle

Other materials:

white sewing thread

cotton binding

scissors

SIZE

The completed linen strip measures 2¼ x 56in (5.5 x 142cm)

Making the sash

To make a sash like this, work on a large piece of linen and cut out the band when the stitching is complete.

Baste a straight line of stitches through the center of the linen as a guide. Working with two strands of red embroidery cotton, stitch the center line that runs through the band. Work at seven stitches to 1in (2.5cm); leave a space the size of one stitch at every seven stitches. Build up the pattern from the center outwards, stitching the border line at the end.

When you have completed the cross stitching, trim the strip to the desired width, turn under a hem around all four edges of the strip and then oversew it with tiny hemming stitches. Finally, at each end of the strip, sew on a 16in (40cm) piece of cotton binding.

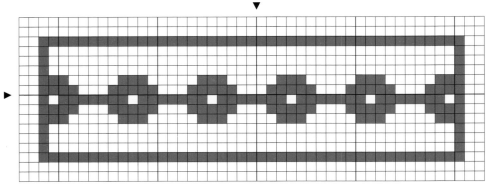

THREAD COLOR

		Anchor	DMC
▨	Red	9046	321

▶ This elegant linen sash is an old-fashioned method of tying towels together.

Laundry bag

This white, cotton drawstring laundry bag has been transformed with the addition of a colorful stitched motif of a milkmaid holding two jugs. The design was inspired by a traditional piece of Czechoslovakian cross stitch, seen at a museum in Prague. Although the motif has a traditional theme, it looks quite modern on a white background with the use of bright red, turquoise, and yellow embroidery cottons. Hang it on the airing cupboard door handle or place it in a corner of the bathroom to bring a smile to the washday chores.

MATERIALS

For the cross-stitch design:

two pieces of white linen, 32 x 28in (80 x 70cm)

vanishing pen

dark-colored cotton

sewing needle

embroidery hoop

2 skeins of red (DMC 817) embroidery cotton

tapestry needle

1 skein each of yellow (DMC 726), blue (DMC 995), and blue (DMC 996) embroidery cotton

Other materials:

scissors

iron

pins

white cotton

sewing machine

tape measure

white cord

SIZE

The completed bag measures 25½ x 27in (66 x 69cm).

Making the laundry bag

As this project is not worked on counted Aida but on linen, it is a project better suited to those with some experience rather than to novice cross stitchers. The careful measuring and marking off on the linen will ensure a good finish. When stretching the linen, make sure that the warp and weft are not distorted in the frame but run straight and true.

Take one of the pieces of linen and, using a vanishing pen, mark the center point 8in (20cm) from the bottom of the fabric; this will be midway between the milkmaid's feet. Work out the distance between the top of the head to the bottom of the feet. Mark these areas off with basting stitches, using a dark cotton thread; these can then be used as guidelines while sewing.

Place the marked linen in an embroidery hoop. Then, using three strands of red embroidery thread, cross stitch the whole outline of the motif before adding the other colors.

When you have finished the cross stitching, remove the linen from the embroidery hoop and iron it flat with a hot iron. Then place it on the second piece of linen, right sides together. Pin, then sew around three sides, including the two long sides, using the sewing machine; leave a 8in (20cm) gap at the top of one of the long sides.

Turn in the opening of the bag by folding over the top by 4in (10cm). Fold under the raw edge and sew down, also remembering to fold under the raw edges from the side. You will now have made a channel at the top of the bag; thread a length of white cord through the gap in the channel and tie the ends of the cord together to form a drawstring for the laundry bag.

▶ A laundry bag like this can be made to any size. The motif can be stitched on to Aida and in turn sewn on to a smaller bag as a patch.

◄ Like many cross-stitch motifs, this milkmaid is perfectly symmetrical. Stitch the entire outline first, as it is one color, and then fill in the other colors afterwards.

THREAD COLORS

		Anchor	DMC
	Red	19	817
	Yellow	295	726
	Blue	410	995
	Blue	433	996

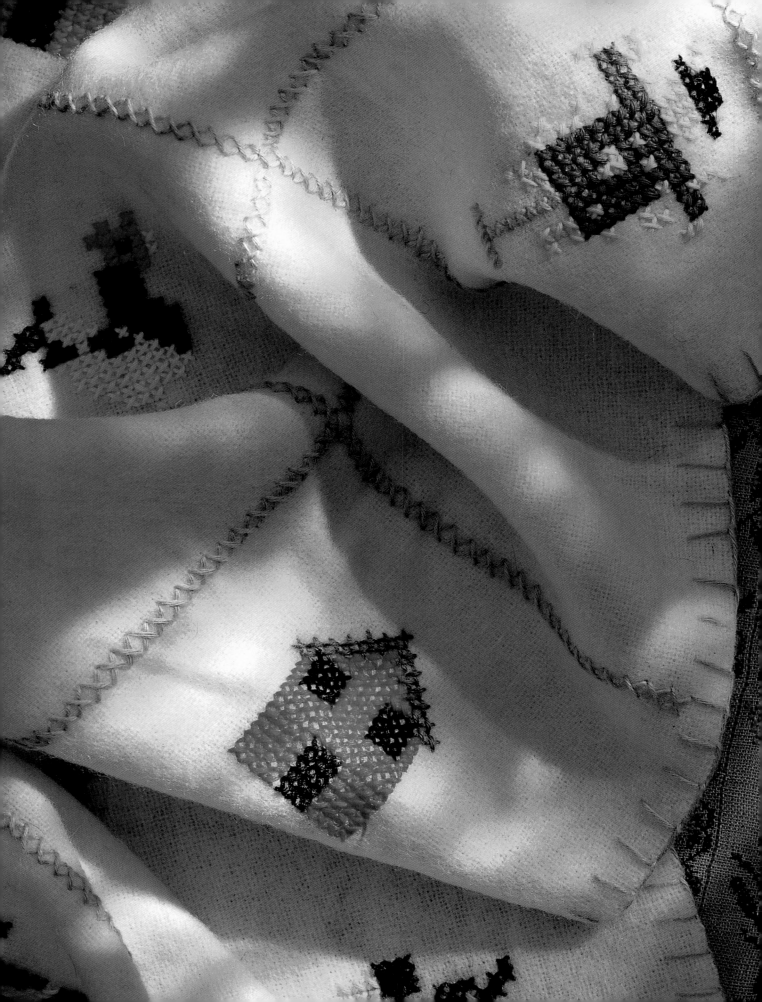

CHILDREN'S ROOMS

*F*rom the ubiquitous sampler to fleecy baby blankets, cross-stitched gifts for children have always been popular, and there is a wide choice of items you can make to brighten your children's rooms.

You can stitch a sampler and create your own personal family heirloom, or make a baby blanket decorated with farmyard animals in bright colors. The novice stitcher can begin with a simple bookmark or paperweight or even stitch a child-sized Christmas stocking.

Farmyard baby blanket

An old blanket has been cut up and made into a charming baby blanket for use in the cot, stroller, bed, or as a comforter. The simple, colorful motifs are easily recognizable as the farmer and his farmyard animals. Although they are not traditional motifs for baby blankets, they do look charming—you could make a game with it and try to get the child to name the animals. This baby blanket makes a great project for both beginners and experienced cross stitchers alike.

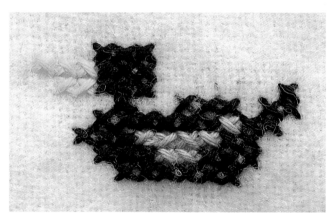

▲ The strong dark colors of this stitched duck motif contrast well with the light background.

◀ This neat red house with its simple black windows and a door in the center is very easy to cross stitch.

MATERIALS

For the cross-stitch design:

cream or off-white blanket fabric, 30 x 36in (75 x 91cm)

tape measure

pins

large tapestry needle

soft cotton embroidery yarn in a mixture of colors: 8 skeins of light green (DMC 2954), 1 skein each of black (DMC 2371), light yellow (DMC 2155), blue (DMC 2826), peach (DMC 2745), green (DMC 2320), brown (DMC 2153), cream (DMC 2727), blue (DMC 2797), red (DMC 2106), mid blue (DMC 2827) (most of these motifs use less than a full skein of yarn)

scissors

waste canvas

dark-colored cotton

sewing needle

tweezers

SIZE

The completed baby blanket measures 31 x 43in (78 x 108cm).

▶ This cozy blanket with its enchanting farmyard motifs can be used throughout a baby's childhood.

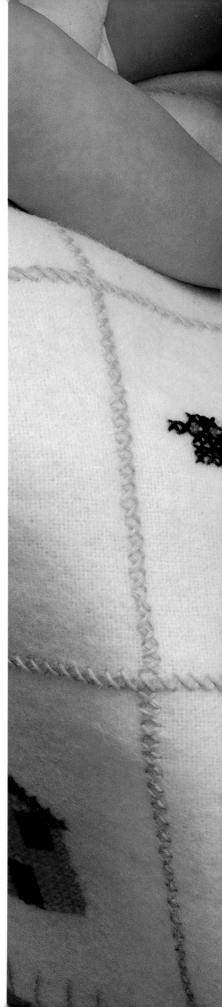

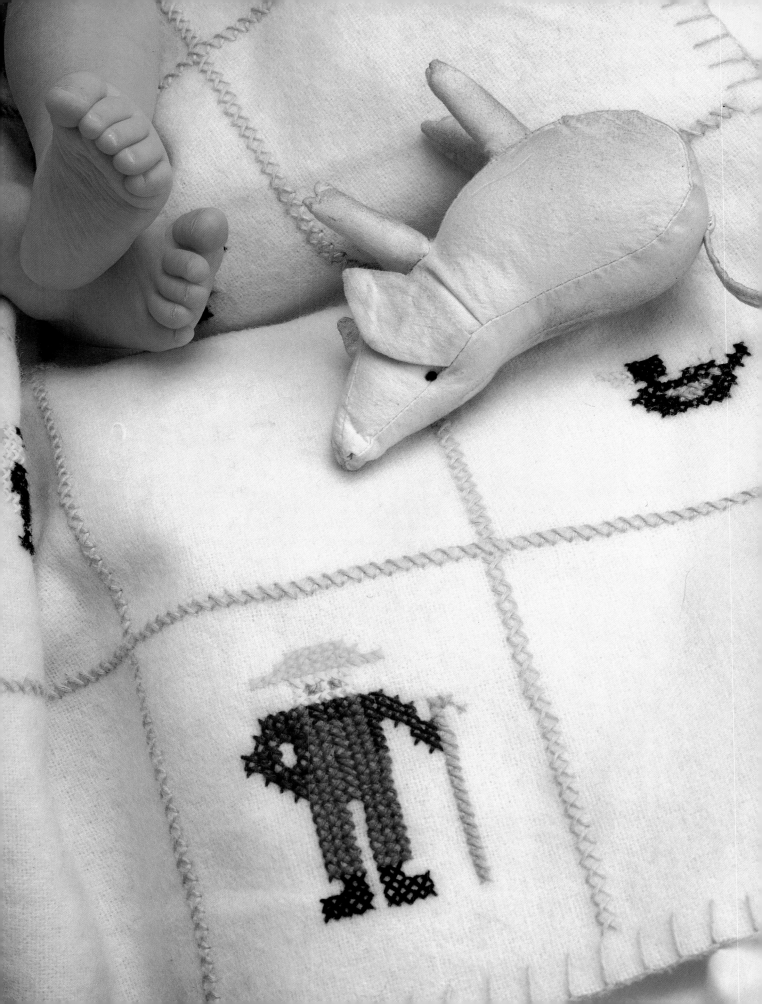

Getting started

Although this blanket has been designed using farmyard motifs, if it is a present for the birth of a new baby or even for an older child it could incorporate letters or the age or birthday of the recipient. These can be found in the Alphabet Charts (see pages 108-11), or on the Traditional Sampler design (see page 104).

◄ This cross-stitched farmer with his heavy boots, oblong head, and brightly colored bib and overalls is an easily recognizable character.

Working the cross stitch

1 Using a tape measure, divide the blanket into 35 squares, each measuring 5¼in (13cm). Mark the corner of each square with pins. Then, using a single strand of green embroidery cotton, cross stitch across and along the blanket, joining up the pin marks, to enclose the 35 squares.

2 Place a small square of waste canvas on to each alternative square on the blanket, and baste central horizontal and vertical lines over each piece; these will be used as guidelines when cross stitching the motifs into place.

3 Following the chart, begin to cross stitch the motifs

through both the waste canvas and the blanket, using two strands of embroidery cotton in the needle. Each motif is very simple and uses a maximum of five colors. Begin with the smallest motif, such as the duck, before moving on to the larger motifs like the farmer and the scarecrow. When you have completed the cross stitching,

carefully pull out the threads of the waste canvas individually with tweezers, to reveal the design on the blanket.

4 **Edging the blanket**
Blanket stitch around the entire edge of the blanket, in the same light green embroidery cotton as used for the cross-stitched squares.

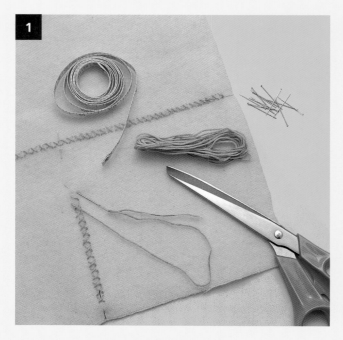

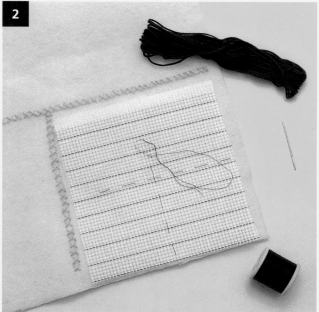

◀ This motif depicts a scarecrow with a yellow head, blue body and top hat, standing on a stalk. Yellow straw sticks out from his body at all angles.

▼ This charming cow has creamy yellow patches and the brightest blue eyes staring out in surprise. Note how simple, yet effective the shape is.

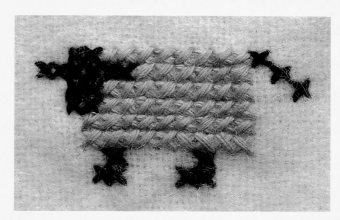

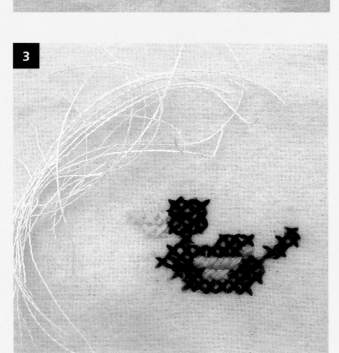

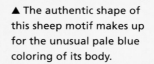

▲ The authentic shape of this sheep motif makes up for the unusual pale blue coloring of its body.

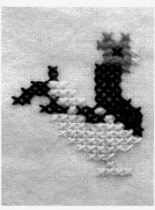

▶ No farmyard would be complete without a rooster. This rooster motif has a very fine red head and comb with bright yellow beak and feet.

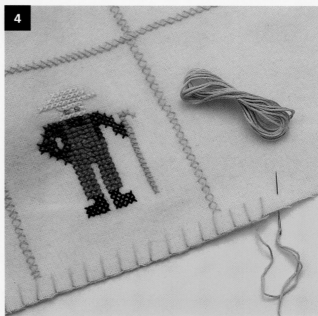

3

4

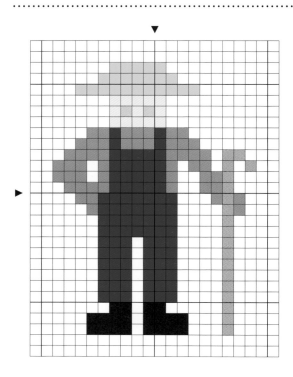

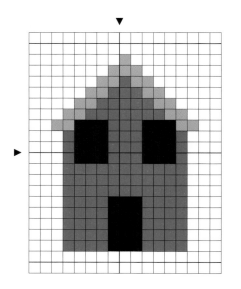

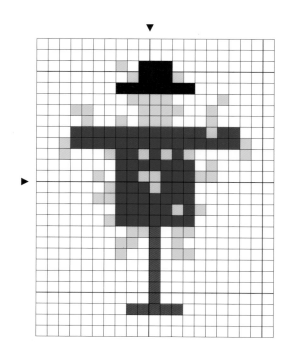

THREAD COLORS

		DMC
	Green	2320
	Black	2371
	Light yellow	2155
	Blue	2826
	Peach	2745
	Brown	2153
	Cream	2727
	Blue	2797
	Red	2106
	Mid blue	2827
	Light green	2954

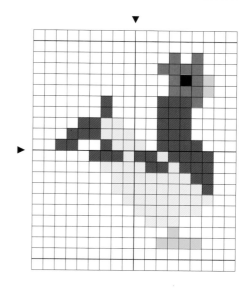

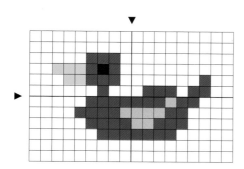

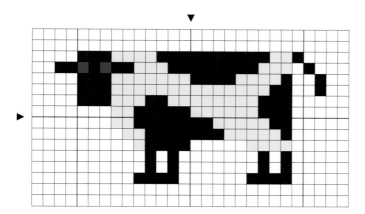

Paperweights

These slightly magnified glass paperweights were just crying out to be filled with an interesting cross-stitched motif. The amusing skier and decorative snowflake designs make them perfect as Christmas gifts, when many families go skiing in the winter snow. You could extend this idea and stitch other snowy motifs, such as a rotund snowman, a snow-covered Christmas tree or a child on a sled, to fit into a paperweight. You could, alternatively, use these motifs to create cross-stitched Christmas cards.

MATERIALS

For the cross-stitch design:

11-count, white Aida

dark-colored thread

sewing needle

embroidery hoop

1 skein of red (DMC 321) embroidery cotton

tapestry needle

Other materials:

glass paperweight

pencil

dressmaker's scissors

SIZE

The completed design measures 4in (10cm) in diameter.

▲ This comic design of a snow-ploughing skier is suitable for all those friends and family who ski.

▶ A traditional snowflake design is an elegant solution for a Christmas paperweight.

▶ Heavy glass paperweights such as these are made especially for cross stitchers. Being small and therefore quick to stitch, they make ideal gifts.

*G*etting started

Being very quick and easy to work, these designs are ideal for a beginner to tackle. Many companies which produce threads and needles also produce decorative accessories such as these paperweights, with all the items needed to fit and cover a piece of cross stitch.

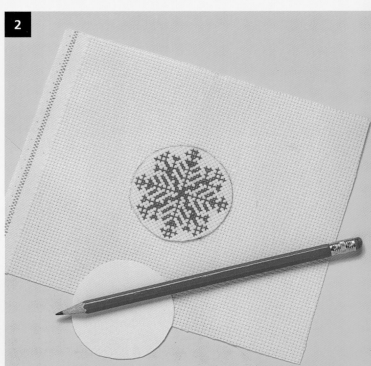

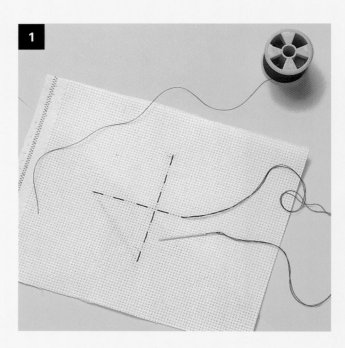

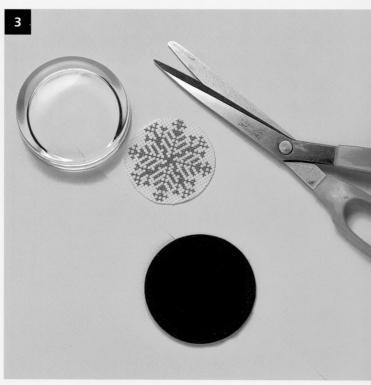

Working the cross stitch

1 Although the motif is small, the Aida needs to be large enough so that it can be held taut in an embroidery hoop. Baste the central points of the design on the Aida with the dark cotton.

2 Cross stitch the snowflake design, working from the center outwards, and using two strands of embroidery cotton. Then, place the circular paper template that comes with the paperweight over the stitched motif, and draw around it with a pencil.

Assembling the paperweight

3 Cut out the circle, following the pencil line. Place the round piece of stitched Aida in the paperweight, face up. Then peel the backing off the green felt disc and stick the felt over the back of the cross stitch to secure.

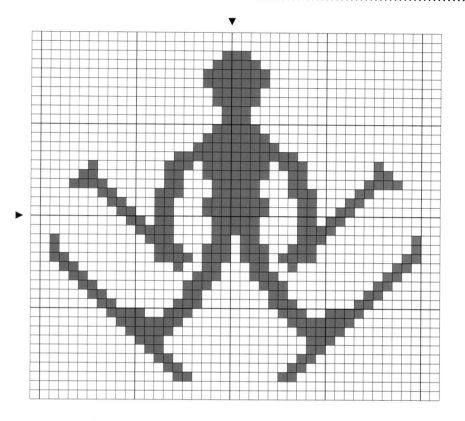

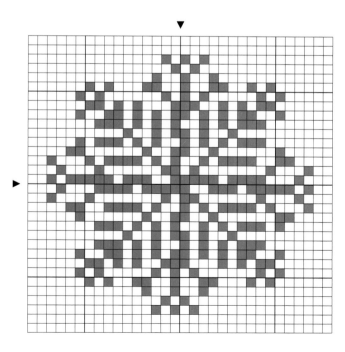

THREAD COLOR

		Anchor	DMC
▬	Red	9046	321

Christmas stocking

Many people make their own Christmas stockings during the festive season, and they can range from old socks to elaborate silk stockings. This stocking has a cross-stitched front which has been sewn on to a fabric backing. The pattern incorporates stars and zigzags, both simple motifs are given a lift by using strong colors. Although the stocking is tiny, it can be scaled up or down depending on the size you want it to be.

MATERIALS

For the cross-stitch design:

dark-colored cotton

sewing needle

waste canvas, size 14

28-count, navy Brittany evenweave

1 skein of yellow (DMC 444) embroidery cotton

tapestry needle

Other materials:

tweezers

scissors

tailor's chalk

pins

blue felt

yellow or blue cord

silk or satin (optional)

SIZE

The completed design measures 6½ x 5in (16.5 x 13cm).

▲ A blue Christmas stocking decorated with yellow stitched stars makes a welcome change from the more usual red and green festive colors.

▶ This miniature Christmas stocking does not take long to stitch, making it ideal for the novice cross stitcher. Fill it with sweets or small toys for a festive surprise.

Getting started

The Christmas stocking shown here is quite tiny and is more for decorative purposes than to be stuffed full of presents. It would look pretty hanging from a Christmas tree or from a mantelpiece. If you wish to make a larger stocking, simply scale up the design to the size you desire. You can also make a sumptuous silk lining in a contrasting color for the stocking if you like.

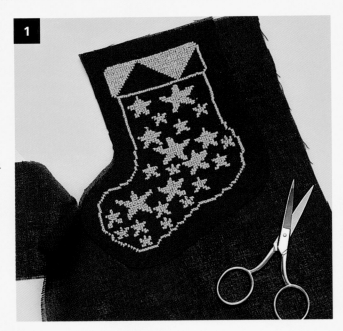

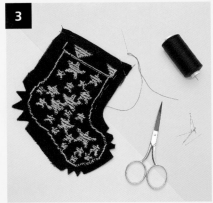

Working the cross stitch

1 Baste the waste canvas on to the evenweave fabric and work the cross stitch through both of them, with two strands of embroidery cotton in the needle. When you have completed the cross stitch, remove the canvas mesh by pulling out the threads one by one with tweezers. Then cut out the cross-stitched stocking, leaving an allowance of 2in (5cm) around all the edges.

Making the stocking

2 Place the stitched stocking on top of a piece of blue felt and draw around it with tailor's chalk. Cut out the chalked shape. Pin, then baste the two stocking pieces together, right sides facing. Turn under the top of each piece and secure them both together with pins at the sides.

3 Sew around the stocking 2in (5cm) in from the edges to secure the two pieces together; leave the top unstitched. Using sharp scissors, cut triangular-shaped notches at the curved edges of the stocking so that the seam will curve easily when you turn the stocking the right way out.

4 Turn the stocking the right way out. Sew a matching cord around the top edge and make a loop for hanging the stocking up. If you wish, you could line the stocking in a contrasting color using a luscious fabric such as silk or satin. Cut two stocking shapes from the fabric and sew together as for the stocking. Place the lining in the stocking, turn under the top edge, and oversew to the top inner edge of the stocking.

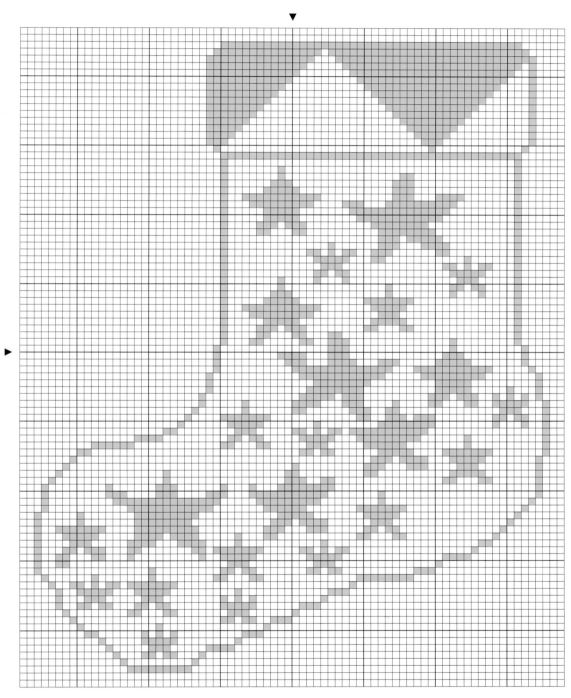

THREAD COLOR

		Anchor	DMC
	Yellow	291	444

Bookmarks

The frayed bookmark was inspired by butterflies; the second bookmark was inspired by ecclesiastical needlework.

Making the bookmarks

To make the butterfly design, begin cross stitching six squares in from the edge on one piece of Aida, using two strands of cotton. Sew the second piece of Aida to the back of the first piece with running stitch around the edge. Fray the edges by pulling out rows of Aida thread.

To make the bird bookmark, begin stitching at one end of the edging strip, three squares from the edge, using two strands of cotton. When complete, fold the edging in half to conceal the back of the stitching. Oversew the sides together. Turn in the raw edges at the top and sew down.

MATERIALS

For the cross-stitch designs:

two pieces of 11-count Aida, 8¾ x 2½in (22 x 6.5cm)

Aida scalloped edging strip, 11 x 2in (28 x 5cm)

1 skein each of dark red (DMC 304), mid blue (DMC 824), dark purple (DMC 791), and maroon (DMC 814) embroidery cotton

tapestry needle

Other materials:

scissors

pins

white sewing cotton

sewing needle

SIZE

The completed designs measure approximately 8¾in (22cm) and 5½in (14cm) long.

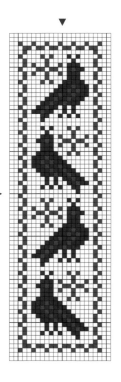

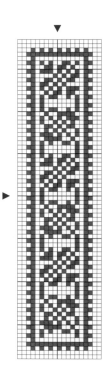

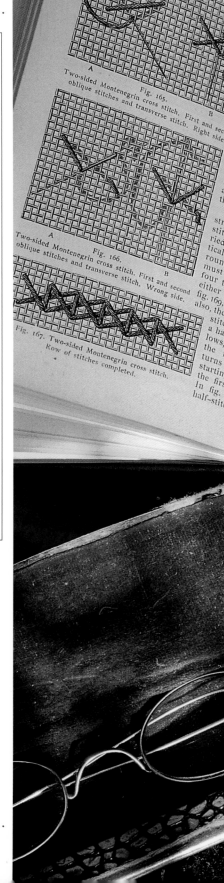

THREAD COLORS

		Anchor	DMC
BUTTERFLY BOOKMARK			
	Dark red	47	304
	Mid blue	164	824
BIRD BOOKMARK			
	Dark purple	178	791
	Maroon	45	814

▶ These stylized bookmarks, featuring butterflies and birds, are simple projects to stitch—ideal for beginners.

Traditional sampler

Borrowed from a friend whose grandmother made it, the sampler opposite was made in 1864 and has been passed down as a family heirloom. A sampler is a perfect symbol for births, marriages, and significant events in a family's history, as we can see from the family tree in this example. Use this as a guide to stitch your own personalized family sampler.

Making the sampler

Although the sampler overleaf appears very difficult to make, if you look at it closely, you will see that it is actually quite simple and it is the variety of motifs and colors that give it substance. There are 14 stitches to an inch (6 stitches to a centimeter), so the work is very small and intricate.

Begin with the border. Using two strands of rose pink embroidery thread, sew tiny running stitches all around the outside edge, leaving a 1in (2.5cm) edge. Then measure in 1in (2.5cm) and sew another line of running stitches all around the edge to form a channel in which to stitch the triangular border.

Using the chart as a guide, partition off each section of the sampler with basting stitches: the first alphabet, the second alphabet, and the set of numbers in between. Once you are satisfied with the partitions, proceed to cross stitch the alphabets in place, using two strands of embroidery thread in the needle. Ensure that the work is held tightly in the embroidery hoop to prevent puckering.

You can replace the name 'J.E. BAWDEN' with another name of your choice, using the Alphabet Charts given on pages 108–11.

Then you can either copy the motifs on the chart, adapt designs from elsewhere, or design your own. If you see a motif you like, trace it on to graph paper, then transfer the outlines into tiny blocks of color, each block representing a single cross stitch.

When you have completed the cross stitching, cut a sheet of cardboard measuring 18 x 11½in (45 x 29cm) and place it centrally on the back of the cross stitch; you should be left with a ½in (1cm) border all around the edge of the sampler. Fold the edges of the linen over and either tape or staple them down on to the cardboard, then place the work in a frame of your choice.

▶ Stitched on fine linen, this decorative sampler depicts numbers, the alphabet, and a range of emblems, trees, and birds, which may have been linked to the stitcher's family.

MATERIALS

For the cross-stitch design:

off-white or beige fine linen, 18¾ x 12½in (47 x 31cm)

1 skein each of rose pink (DMC 3731), dusky blue (DMC 518), light khaki green (DMC 524), creamy pink (DMC 224), soft red (DMC 347), light blue (DMC 3755), dove grey (DMC 932), navy blue (DMC 311), olive green (DMC 3362), khaki green (DMC 936), apple green (DMC 3364), beige (DMC 3045)

tapestry needle

tape measure

dark-colored cotton

sewing needle

embroidery hoop

Other materials:

scissors

cardboard, 18in x 11½ (45 x 29cm)

masking tape or stapler

frame

SIZE

The completed design measures 45 x 29cm (18 x 11½in).

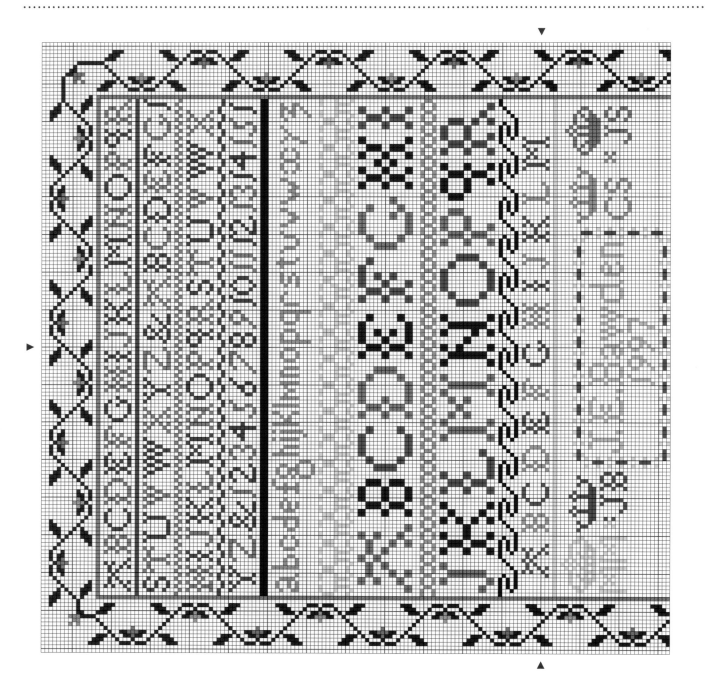

THREAD COLORS

		Anchor	DMC
	Rose pink	38	3731
	Dusky blue	168	518
	Light khaki green	858	524
	Creamy pink	893	224
	Soft red	13	347
	Light blue	140	3755
	Dove grey	343	932
	Navy blue	148	311
	Olive green	263	3362
	Khaki green	846	936
	Apple green	260	3364
	Beige	888	3045

*L*ower case alphabet

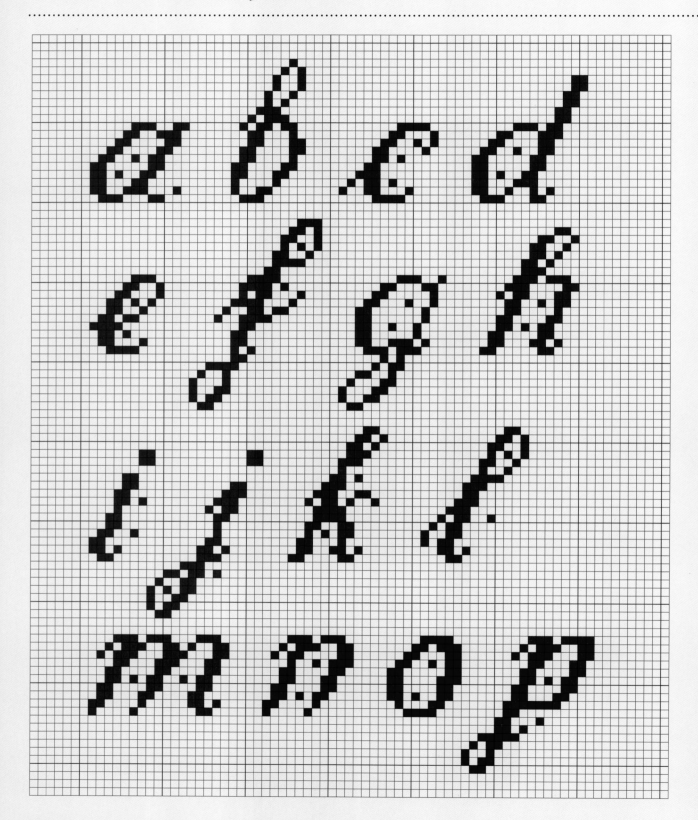

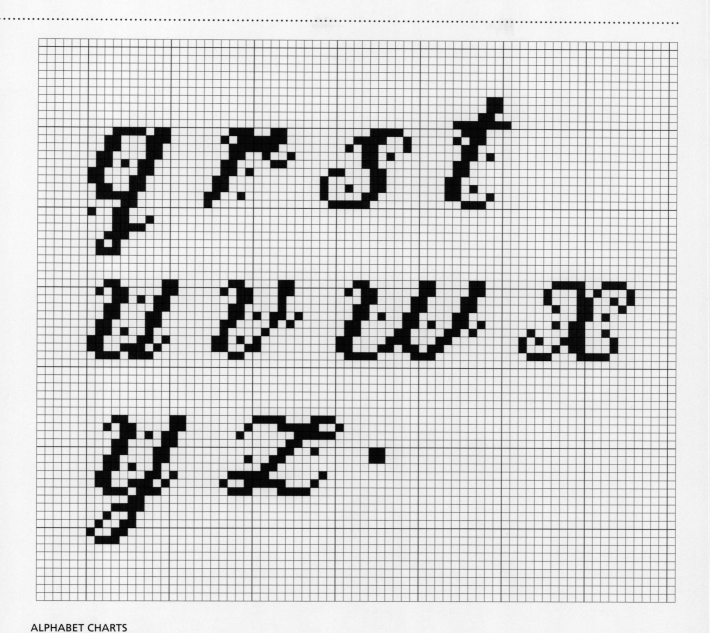

ALPHABET CHARTS
Refer to these alphabet
charts to personalize your
monogrammed pillowcases
(see page 54), drawstring
bags (see page 64),
traditional sampler (see page
104), or your own cross
stitched design. Choose from
capital letters, lower case
letters, or use a combination
of both.

Upper case alphabet

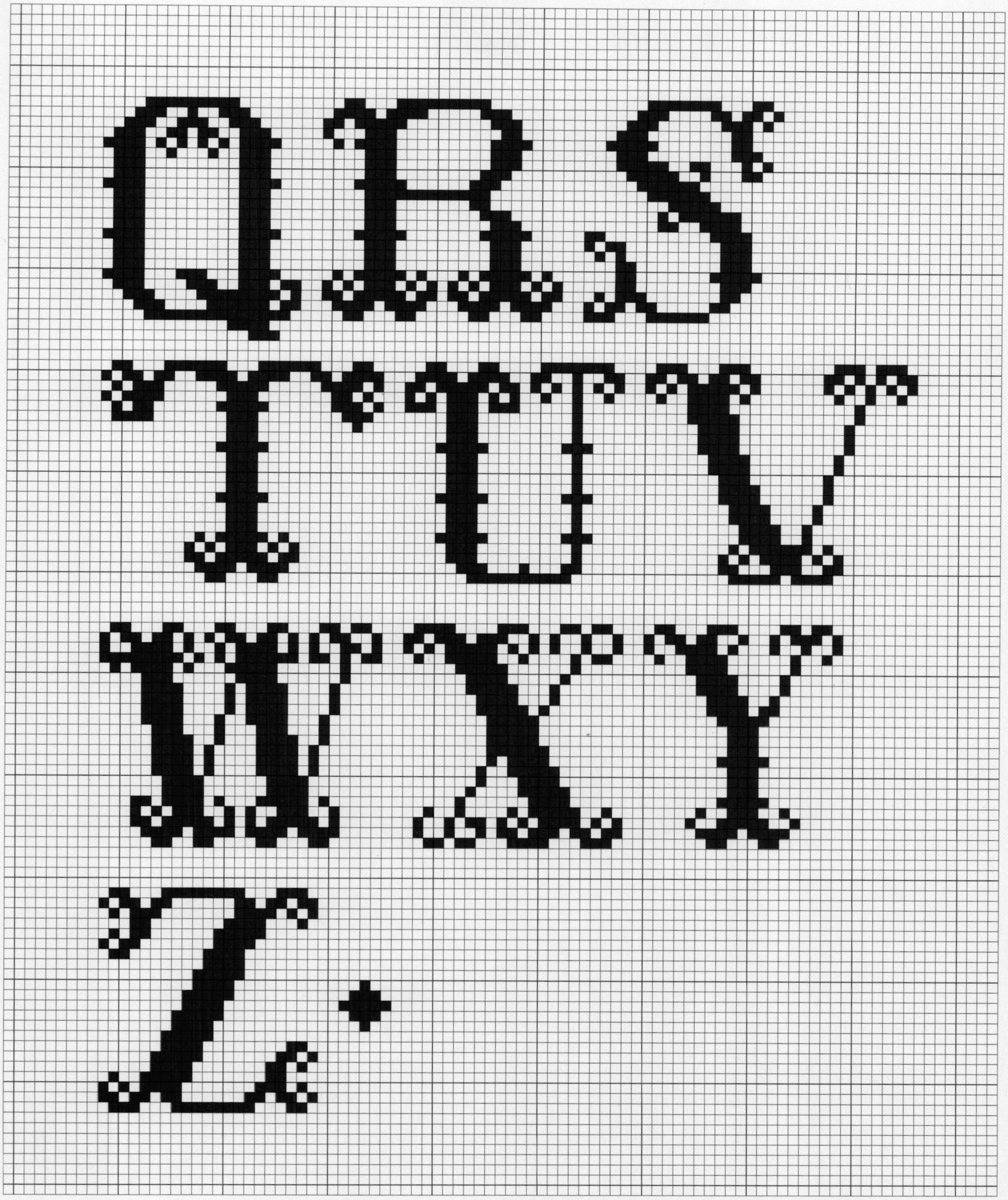

ACKNOWLEDGMENTS

MANY THANKS TO THE FOLLOWING

For all embroidery threads, fabrics, and needlework equipment:

DMC Creative World
Pullman Road
Wigston
Leicester
LE8 2DY
Tel: 0116 2811040

The stitchers:

Naseem Akhtar
Esther Burt
Marilyn McAuslam

For loaning antique pieces:

Val Ferguson
Ivana Jenkins